Who Likes Short Shorts

Pete Sortwell

ISBN-13:978-1493715640
ISBN-10:149371564X

DEDICATION

For Andy Rivers and all at Byker Books. Thanks for giving me my first experience of being published.

ACKNOWLEDGEMENTS

I wouldn't be able to get my work into your hands if it wasn't for the help of the team I employ, they work extremely hard to make sure what ends up on your kindle is a high quality. These people are:

Julie Lewthwaite, for her continued sterling work on turning my ramblings into something that I can charge money for. http://www.mlwritingservices.co.uk/

Graham D. Lock, for the excellent covers he's provided me. http://www.peopleperhour.com/people/graham-d/animator-graphic-designer-and-illu/177926

I can't recommend these people enough.

INTRODUCTION

I first started writing short stories back in 2010, shortly after I'd written the first three chapters of my first novel, *So Low, So High*. I've always been a fan of Adrian Mole, brilliantly written by Sue Townsend, and I remembered how he thinks he is a brilliant writer and spends years working on the most dire novels, only to discover much later that they're rubbish. I didn't want to do that and during the first four months of my writing I was in the stage that I think most people go through – I was doing it in private and not daring to tell anyone. I still wonder why we all do that, but I suppose it comes down to confidence, not that writing is some dirty activity that you must take to your grave. The fact is if you want to be successful then people need to read your work and, crucially, like it.

So, what I did was stalk my favourite writer, Danny King, on Amazon one day and I found some books that he'd featured in as a short story writer. The books were called *Radgepacket* and published by Byker Books, who had also published one of his novels. I think I looked at their website and saw they had an open submission for the next in the series of short story collections. Not knowing anything about the writing process at all, I assumed 'editor' meant 'general dogsbody', someone who would completely tidy up the short story I'd written and probably want to talk to me over the phone to tell me how brilliant I was.

Wrong.

I got a reply thanking me for my submission, but suggesting I take the time to look at the technical side of writing. 'Ed' as I came to know him also suggested a website – Chapter79 – that I could go to to learn this stuff, which I did. I went over, put the short story up and got some feedback from my peers.

My mistake had been to assume that all stories needed to be in third person. This wasn't the style I'd written the first three chapters of my novel in and it isn't a style I am comfortable with now. Shortly after that I also posted those first three chapters, albeit in a very rough state, and a guy called Ian Ayris posted to let me know how much he'd enjoyed reading them and said that I definitely had a voice that made him want to read more.

It was a few months into my membership of C79 that I realised I still had a month left before the deadline for *Radgepacket 5*, so what with having done a lot of exercises, found my style and also gotten a few more chapters done, I decided I would write a story using the main character from the book, Simon Brewster.

The rest, as they say, is history, I spent a month on the story, I made it as good as I possibly could myself, I got a friend, Hannah, from C79 to proofread and edit it for me, and I sent it off to Byker Books with a day or so to spare, although I didn't put my phone number at the bottom this time. That was September 2010. It was January 2011 that I heard I was in.

Now, I've signed contracts for books, I've sold over twelve thousand of my self-published books, and I've enjoyed other achievements in my writing 'career', too, but I can honestly say, nothing has beaten that feeling of being published for the first time. I finally realised I was worthy of someone else's time and money. To be honest, it is probably the thing that helped me gain the confidence to carry on with the novel, and then spend a fair amount of money getting it properly edited once I was done. I can't thank the guys at Byker Books enough for the boost they gave me back in the early days and I know it isn't just me they've supported. There are several guys I know who are now signed up to publishing contracts and/or doing well in their self-publishing. So thanks, Byker Books, for that.

In case you're wondering, the original short story was eventually re-written and is now the backdrop to a sub plot in *So Low, So High;* it's featured here under the title 'One Flew Over The Policeman's Bonnet'.

That's about it for now. I hope you enjoy what you read here. As well as the short stories I've also included samples from my other books, so you can follow my writing journey from the very first story right up to my latest self-published book.

All the best,

Pete

PETE SORTWELL

CONTENTS

SHORT STORIES

PETE SORTWELL

NOANG LISH

This ain't a bad job really, I get to sit on my sleeping bag all day. Except for getting up and flicking a few switches every six hours. They say after I have done six cycles of the crop I'll have paid my way, then I'll be taken off to the nearest local authority and dropped off. From there it's easy street for me, free house, money from the government, more if I say I am a child and disabled. I have a script.

'Ah yam sik steen noang lish chile, chile.'

Quang, the man who collected me, told me this, says he has done it loads of times. It's his job. A few of my friends have done this and told me it is a good way to get out of the country and start looking out for the elders that are stuck there. Mother was sad to see me go but Father looked at me like a man when I told him of my decision to go. Quang promised my mother I would be looked after. We shared a joke at how silly the rich country was, just giving money away. I know it is naughty to be doing it, but Quang says there is very little chance of getting caught. Quang said the police here even feed you. I know the English word for police.

There is everything to gain. It will save them taking my sister, too, she does not want to leave and I am scared they will hurt her.

The stuff I have to grow really smells. Makes me feel funny, too. I have put a sheet up over the door of the small room where I rest between turning these huge fans and funny shaped lights on and off. I only get three hours sleep at a time as the four rooms of the place have different rules on when I need to change the settings. It takes about half an hour to do it all then I go and sit back on my sleeping bag and put the sheet up.

The men that picked me up from Mum and Dad's house were friendly and nice. They brought me cigarettes and chocolate for the journey. The men that picked me up from here were not so nice and one just shouted at me. A Vietnamese man explained my job and the rules. I must not to go out of the place, I must not to write anything down, I must remember the timings of the lighting, and I must practise my script in English. He was not as nice as the men in Vietnam.

The only time people come to the house is at night, every few weeks. I never know when they are coming exactly, but it is after I have bagged up the latest crop. I get jumpy at any noises in the night. Just in case it's them. They don't speak to me nicely like Quang said they would.

I get hungry often. The plants here can be eaten, but I always sleep more when I do that. I eat tins of food that the men bring. I don't like being here, but I need to provide for my family, they are good people.

I think about them a lot.

I was thinking about them today, actually, when there was

banging downstairs then lots of men came in screaming. I was so frightened, until I heard the words I understood.

'Police! Police!'

I only know one thing to say to them.

'Ah yam sik steen noang lish chile chile.'

PETE SORTWELL

HERO

In my area we have this little corner shop cum Post Office, you know the one, where the local centre it's in used to have separate shops for everything – a butcher's, newsagent, grocer, Post Office and pub. Then Tesco came along and wiped out most small businesses in a thirty mile radius, like some kind of nuclear blast. These areas then shut everything except one shop. If they were really lucky then they got left with a shop and a pub. So the 'local shop' was born – a scaled down supermarket with higher prices, but a free funny smell. Some of them, like the one I was in, had little wooden shacks erected inside to act as Post Offices to dish out the dole money and pensions to the local workshy and coffin dodgers.

I'm just a regular working guy, skint like everyone else at the moment; I don't earn much and they cut my hours at the factory. About a year ago I'm stood in the queue for the Post Office waiting to send off some of my unwanted tat to some idiot off the Internet, minding my own, being patient, tasting the air, that sort of thing, when in comes some trampy looking guy from the estate. Simon's his name. He lives in the flats near the main road – everyone knows him. He's one of the local smackheads.

First of all he just goes behind the counter and starts necking the vodka off the shelf until Devina, the owner, manages to keep some of her stock by pushing him to the floor. I'm just watching the show at this point, not getting involved. Simon starts shouting up from the floor that his back and neck hurt, Devina's claiming she never pushed him. Before we can all get our stories straight, two young scoundrels from the estate run in and go straight behind the counter and reach around the back of the tills and pop the drawer open.

Sneaky fuckers, I think to myself, where'd they learn how to do things like that? I've never seen it on the TV.

Simon is still on the floor and as Devina heads for the lads, he grabs her legs. It don't matter anyway as they've emptied the tills of all the notes and are heading over towards the Post Office lean-to, the bigger of the two just does a running jump at the door of the structure, shaking it like jelly. There's a lot of panicking in the queue; the woman in front of me starts crying and the woman in front of her is looking to the ceiling and praying in a language which isn't one of the two I speak, English or Bullshit.

I'm a little scared, to be completely honest. I challenge any man reading this to say he wouldn't be with all the banging, shouting and panic going on around him.

The first thought that goes through my mind is run, sod everyone else and just look after number one, but something inside me stops me and my ego kicks in. I've always wanted to be someone. Not super rich or harassed in the street, famous or anything, just ... someone, you know? Have people nod at you out of respect, talk about you in a nice, respectful way when you're out the room, remember you when you're gone, that sort of thing. That's probably why I did what I did, why I risked being on this earth, why I risked never seeing my mum again, never feeling the joy that being a father brings, never being able to shout abuse randomly and without retribution in the street as a pensioner.

I check the door; there's no other members of this outfit blocking the exit. Then something inside me, call it bravery or stupidity, makes me dig my heels in against my original plan of leaving the pool of crying grannies to it. I look about for a weapon. 'Ah ha,' I say excitedly and grab a tin of mixed veg.

Before I know what I'm doing I've hurled the bomb of canned goods at the two likely lads, who are kicking the door and screaming at Devina's husband, Tufan, on the other side to 'Open the fucking door, you cunt.'

The tins miss, but pound against the thick plastic front and make the lads turn their attention disorders towards me.

'You fucking want some, mate?' the ginger one with the lame eye shouts across.

'Err,' I reply. I mean what do you say to that? In that situation! It's gotta be only nutters that turn round and say 'Yeah, alright mate, I'll have some.' It just sounds bent.

'You're not my type,' I shout back, launching a few more tins, all of which miss. They cause the rest of the people standing in front of me to drop to the floor as the lads start hurling them back, knocking things off the shelves all around us.

'Stop it,' one older lady, scared out her wits, says from near my feet.

Just then one of their cans catches me right between the tit and shoulder blade. Arrrgh! That fucking smarts.

It isn't my throwing arm, though, so I just continue to belt tins at the two perps.

It seems all their attention is now focused on taking me down now, rather than kicking fuck out of the poor excuse for a Post Office employee.

'Yea blud, you step to us you're gunna get messed up,' the boss-eyed one shouts at me.

The cock behind starts heading my way. 'You want some? You fucking want some?' he says, moving forward with his arms outstretched, leaving himself wide open and much closer.

WHACK! A tin smacks him right on the forehead and he goes down.

'Aha! Got him!' I yell, forgetting I am in the middle of a robbery and not at a funfair.

I feel like doing a little dance and picking the granny up off the floor in front of me and kissing her in celebration. My elation is short-lived, though, as I feel an almighty pain in my right ankle. I look down and Simon is fucking biting me. Arrrgh!

'Get off, you stinking junkie,' I shout down at him. He doesn't listen, so is rewarded with not one, but two, tins to the side of the face, leaving him out cold, bleeding on the floor next to the granny.

I look up and the other assailant is just standing like a rabbit in the headlights. I'm weighing up what to do now, sit down and cry from the pain in my leg or just keep pelting these tin grenades. I choose the latter and just keep hurling them; BANG BANG BANG they go, as they all miss and hit the Perspex safety glass. They are having the right effect, though, as he looks like he is going to cry. 'You're out your league, son, just give it up and get on the floor,' I order him.

'No, you'll knock me out with a can if I do that,' he shouts back, guessing my plan.

'Well, you'll save yourself the fall, then, won't you!' I say in mocking tones as I lob one more, aiming for the Perspex this time just to create a bit more panic in him. DUFF!

'Fucking hell, mate, leave it out, I surrender, OK?'

This is where it all goes pear shaped; I show weakness, I'm not one for watching someone suffer and as I look at the fear in his eyes, I crumble inside and come down off whatever adrenaline high I've been on, chucking the tins.

I put the tin I'm gripping tightly in my hands down and start to approach him.

'Call the police, will you?' I shout over to Devina.

'Already pressed the button,' she replies smugly.

I approach the robber, who looks no more than sixteen. God knows what I think I'm going to do when I get there, hold him down or something, but it doesn't get that far.

I'm so pleased with myself for stopping the robbery single-handed that I don't see the knife he's pulled out until it's well on its way towards my gut.

I don't know why, but I put my hands over my stomach to block it. I think it was just a knee jerk reaction. The first blow hits my wrist, which makes my hands, which by now have a mind of their own, move away; I don't have time to try and shake the pain away before the next thrust gets me in the stomach. I feel an awful pain instantly.

I've seen on Crimewatch that some people think a stabbing feels just like a punch, but not in my case; it fucking hurts like a punch on the outside and a hot sharp thing cutting open my stomach lining on the inside. I start falling as soon as the knife comes out, I don't have much time to think before the next few digs go in and out my left arm.

I'm on the deck by the time the stabbing stops. I have eight wounds in total.

After the only surviving member of the gang has had it away, Devina comes over and asks me if I'm OK.

'Not really, girl, I'm in a bad way,' I reply. That is the last thing I remember before I black out.

The police dragged Simon and the ginger from the scene, as they hadn't stirred from their snooze by the time they'd arrived. I think Devina or Tufan had given their bollocks a good stamping while they were out cold, the court papers stated they had injuries there, too, and I know my aim with the tins wasn't that good. Sadly.

Devina had tried her best to stop the bleeding with towels before the ambulance crew arrived, but wasn't able to stop the stomach wound and I had to take a fast trip in the back of an ambulance, which I can tell you now is not as comfortable as it looks on the TV. I lost five pints of blood that day.

I stayed in hospital for a week in total. I'm told on the first day Simon and the ginger were in the same ward, both cuffed to their beds.

It's funny, I never thought at the time I might die. I have since, though, the nightmares still scare the living shit out of me. The hospital told me it would happen, post-traumatic stress they call it.

It took six months for the case to go to court. With my statement and witness testimony and, of course the CCTV, Simon got three months, Mikey – the one who made it away – got seven for attempted robbery and attempted murder, and the ginger got four for attempted robbery.

Me? I got six months off work, post-traumatic stress, negative feedback off the buyer of the item I was posting that day, and my name remembered by Devina and her husband every time I go in their shop now.

The best thing that came out of it, though, was the newspaper article. It read:

HERO STOPS ARMED ROBBERS

Yeah, I was publicly named as a hero.

Just what I always wanted.

PETE SORTWELL

LOSE-LOSE

Waiting outside the court there's been nothing on my mind more than letting the scumbag get the comeuppance he deserves. If the great British justice system can't serve justice, I will.

I'd been inside the courtroom, of course. A two year suspended sentence he'd been given. That basically meant he wouldn't go to prison at all for what he did. A day in court, a couple of hours in the cells, and he's deemed to have paid his debt to society. Well, he hasn't paid his debt to my dead wife and baby yet.

This country does nothing for the victims of crime. He chose to get behind the wheel of his motor after six pints, he chose to drive it down the high street at sixty miles an hour. No one, least of all my loved ones, chose to have a red Fiesta drive over them, causing horrific injuries.

Getting the call was one of the worst moments of my life. I can't remember putting the phone down or leaving the office. I remember getting to the scene to find the emergency services lifting the car off my wife. There was blood everywhere. My daughter was found in someone's garden, she died from head injuries. My wife was in such a bad state, almost cut in half. It would have been a painful death. That's what this cunt will be getting, too. Peter Andrews, a lawyer, no less. No wonder they let him off. The judge said he'd have to suffer for the rest of his life; I don't suppose he knew how short that would be.

I'd had the conversations with my parents, of course, they begged me not to do it and waste another life. I, of course, agreed not to, but in the back of our minds I think we all knew I was lying. Killing this guy is the only way I will die anything close to happy.

He comes out, all smiles and relief. His family in tow. This just makes me all the more angry. How dare he? I wasn't going to do it in front of his kids, but I can't help it. I run over from the bench I've been waiting on. I'll always remember the look on his face as the broken bottle I'm holding comes towards his face. It's a look of shock. The impact isn't what I expected, it's firmer; I expect the bottle to break up more, but it doesn't, it just goes deep into his face. The plan was to pull it out, but it seems like it'll hurt more if I leave it in. I pull the knife out my belt and go to work on the vital organ areas with that. There's screaming and at one point a woman jumps on my back, but she's light enough to throw off.

The police come, of course. I knew they would. Cells, court, his kids and wife looking at me, prison, Mum crying, and then numbness.

Killing him was easy.

It's living with it that's hard.

SO LOW, SO HIGH

As I'm stood up here, for a few split seconds at a time I wonder if I'm doing the right thing. I'm pretty sure I am. These bastards need to learn that they can't keep fobbing people like me off. They can't and they won't. It ends now. Once this hits the news, that'll show them.

Today I was in there telling the doctor how bad things had got again. For a moment I thought he was going to help me.

'Here, Jed, take these, you'll feel much better.'

Brilliant, I thought, s*ome relief from the voices and noise I can never switch off.*

As I reached over to take the prescription from the Doctor, he continued.

'They can take up to two weeks to start working.' Then he sat back in his chair smiling like he'd actually helped me.

'Two weeks!? TWO FUCKING WEEKS!' I yell, standing up.

'Please, Mr Collins, it is really effective medication,' he starts to say, but I cut him off with more screaming and shouting.

'You bastard doctors have no idea, DO YOU!?'

He keeps trying to butt in but I'm not having it and in the end his desk gets turned over. He must have pressed some kind of panic button because before me or the voices have planned our next move a deafening alarm is going off. So I do what I always do when I'm scared – run.

As I belt it back through the waiting room and past reception, people are bottle necking trying to get out. Old, young, women, the lot are pushed to the ground as I make my way past them and out into the car park. I can hear sirens so it's then I decide to head up here, to the roof. By the time I've managed to clamber up, most people have gone back into the surgery. A child sees me, though, and points me out to his mum. She must have told the staff inside because within a few minutes there are nurses, doctors and the braver of the patients all in the car park, all looking up to me.

'I'll do it,' I call down trying to make them scared. If this gets in the press, they'll be sorry. They'll have to do something other than dish out pills that don't work, then. I can see the headlines now: MAN JUMPS FROM DOCTOR'S ROOF AFTER BEING REFUSED TREATMENT.

And it'll serve them right.

'Jed, come down from there, we'll help you,' one of the nurses calls up to me.

'How?' I reply, only to see her starting to confer with the doctor standing next to her. I can't trust anyone. They're all liars.

I can see right down the lane from here. The police and the fire brigade are heading down. The voices tell me it's the right thing to do. So, much to the horror of everyone watching, I just jump.

The landing went as expected.

'You must be mad,' says the WPC as she looks down at me hanging half-in and half-out of the hedge I'd aimed to land in.

'I might be mad, but I'm not bloody stupid,' I tell her, looking back up at the single storey doctor's surgery.

PETE SORTWELL

WeighTWATcherS

I always have to stand next to the weirdos, on the Tube or in the Post Office. Even if I sit on a town centre bench I'm absolutely guaranteed to get a 'class A' nutter introduce themselves to me and talk about their latest medication. Tonight's no different. I'm in the queue of Weightlosswatchers, sandwiched between the two most boring people this town has ever produced, and that's saying something. They'd give an aspirin a headache.

'It's ridiculous. I mean, I haven't even got a car and they're charging me for the whole year's insurance,' the guy is saying.

'I know, they make you sign up for a whole year, how do they know that you'll keep the car for the full year? You should be able to cancel. I agree,' his partner in boredom tells him.

It's all I can do to point out that most normal people don't smash their car up on the way for secret midnight McDonald's on third party insurance. If you're into late night driving to feed your burger addiction, at least go for 'fully comp'. It makes sense if you think about it.

I don't really want to be here. I'm compelled to be, though.

The missus needs me here. She isn't even that fat. A bit porky, but nothing that calls for all this. I don't like clubs like this. Fat clubs are just sex clubs for bloaters. They just sit around jamming health bars up each other and licking jam rings suggestively. Barry told me he'd seen it when he looked through the window once. I'm not going to let any of these whales harpoon my missus though.

'So I counted out seven chips and just added them to the Weightlosswatchers' pizza,' the bird behind me tells Mr Dull, causing me to offer her my place in the queue, which she readily accepts, but it doesn't quieten her down. I consider sticking the pen I was given into one of my ears, just to cut out fifty per cent of the utter tripe these two barrels are compelled to share with each other.

It's busy here tonight, at least seventy people. This queue is long, I should have come earlier. The wife's sitting down now. She looks upset, maybe one of the lard arses has offered her a go on his banana. I'll have to stop getting distracted by these two.

It's funny how the thoughts of killing people can take your mind off the task in hand, isn't it? I get it all the time. In Tesco I can get totally engrossed in what to do to a woman that's been stood waiting for ages, then decides to fish her purse out of her bag right at the end of the process. They can never find the purse without emptying everything they own onto the counter, then they have to sort through photos of their fish and points cards for shops they haven't been to in years. After I've finished judging, hurting and killing her in my head, I forget to get my fucking money out, too. Other people are just a pain in the arse and these greedy cunts are the worst of the lot.

By the time I finally get round to the scales, the wife's made it to the seats. I can see her from here, though. I wonder what's upset her. I hope this speccy cow I'm about to speak to hasn't done it. There'll be trouble if she has. I'll kick her stand over later, just in case it was.

'Take your shoes off, then step on the scales please, Mr ...?'

'Kendall,' I tell her, taking off my first shoe. My feet fucking stink. She tries her hardest not to turn her nose up, but with the gas northbound there's no way she can avoid it.

'Let's just do it with shoes on this week, shall we?' she tells me, stopping my arm from taking the other shoe off and causing me to wobble on one leg as I try to steady myself.

We go through the pointless process of the weigh in. I might be a little chunky, but I don't care about it. I'm here for one reason and one reason only, for *her*.

I weigh in at fourteen stone. As I get off the scales Hilary addresses me.

'So what brings you here?'

'That,' I tell her, pointing at the digital screen of the scales that is still displaying my weight.

'Oh, just here to feel better about yourself, then?' she asks me, taking me for one of these other comfort eating bloaters.

She then hands me a little folder to keep my thoughts on eating in or something; I don't know, I've stopped listening.

I take a seat at the back, away from the boring people. The wife looks like she's stopped crying now and she has her mates with her, so I just hang at the back and keep an eye out from the rear. There's a fair amount of chunkers in the queue waiting to get patronised by the leader behind me. I can hear all their weights from here. They might as well put a huge screen up so we can all see. It would be more motivational if people were mocked and laughed at for being Big Macs.

The meeting finally starts. Hilary starts going on about how exercise can help people lose weight, who didn't fucking know that? Half the losers here didn't seem to. A particularly huge lady in front of me puts her elbow into her mate's folds and whispers, 'Here, Vic. You know that? I didn't.' Clearly you did, you just ignored it because you like cake in and around your mouth.

It gets even more painful as Hilary, who seems to have few social skills and a poor grasp of when a crowd has given as much as it can, starts singling people out and asking them what exercise they think would be good. Which is a fucking stupid question from the word go. Any exercise is good, unless it's running through a primary school with an AK47.

Some pig in the second row gets the first go at public humiliation.

'Mrs Brown. What do you do?' Hilary asks.

'Er, er,' Mrs Brown says, realising a smile isn't going to get her out of this one. She's got to answer, it's gone well past the point of awkwardness.

'Walking my cat?' Mrs Brown says, causing me to snort the

cold I've been carrying round down my top.

'Shit,' I vocalise without meaning to, wiping the snot from my jumper.

'Mr Kendall, wha …?' That's as far as Hilary gets. The wife turns round and sees me, as does her mate.

'You bastard! You know you're not supposed to be within a hundred yards of her! Someone call the police,' her mate shouts.

The game's up.

At least I got to take Hilary's stand down with me when the gang of beach balls all started practicing the exercising theory by charging at me and pinning me down till the Old Bill got there.

PETE SORTWELL

MULTI-STOREY

I've only been here an hour and already I hate it. My first job in five years and it's boring me to fuck already. Don't you just hate the way the job advert and the lying bastards that interview you lie about how good it is? I do.

'Security operative' is the title of the job I applied for. Well, as I'm sat near the barriers in this Portakabin that's smaller than my understairs cupboard, I am not doing much fucking operating. The guy that interviewed me, David Foster, told me I'd have no time to be bored; that it would be varied work. Well, half an hour in and with no lunch left, I can tell you that's bollocks.

Most of the car park is shut as they are renovating the complex attached to it. Only the bottom level remains open. Inside, only the cinema is open. The casino closed early this morning for the last time until the whole place reopens and makes the town's residents' lives far less dull than mine seems at the moment.

One car I've seen tonight. One! There's only three more inside and one of them is a van that will no doubt be here for the night.

I had hoped I'd get to move about to a different location tonight but there's been no talk of it. Paul, a fat guy that supervises the operatives, dropped me off and just said he'd be round every few hours to check on me.

'And don't let them fuckin' skateboarders in,' Paul shouted out the van window as he left.

Hardly fucking varied, is it? I've got a good mind to let the fucking emo weirdos in to skate all they like, just for entertainment.

I might run to the parade round the corner later, see if there's any takeaways. I'll never see the night out on an empty stomach, especially once I've smoked the two joints I brought with me.

Deciding to have a little wander, I walk over to the back entrance. How they can call this place a 'complex' I have no idea. It comprises a fleapit of a casino, two crappy fast food joints and the world's smallest cinema. I've seen bigger screens in people's homes.

As I get to the door I spot an alley to the left that leads past the back of a shop and out to the street. I stand just into it, so I can still see my Portakabin, and I spark up.

'Giz a bit, then, mate." A girl's voice behind me makes me jump out my skin and the voice turns to a laugh. I turn round to see some ugly emo girl standing behind me.

'Christ! Don't sneak up on people, girl,' I tell her. 'And no, I ain't giving you any.'

'Come on, honey, I'd make it worth your while,' she says,

getting closer and breathing alcohol all over me. I turn my face and screw it up like someone's just dropped a silent but violent. Ugly is not the word. She looks like a gargoyle in leather, after having just being run over by a make up truck. Christ, She'd give Viagra a floppy. I pull wildly on the joint until there are about four goes left and turn back to the girl.

'Will you fuck off if I give you this?'

'Sure,' Emo girl says, taking the joint out my fingers and stumbling off down the alley again. I suddenly don't feel so peckish now.

I waste an hour running my phone battery down to nothing on Beach Racer 2, then the next five minutes wondering what happened to Beach Racer 1. I've never seen it. I go back to being bored and hating myself a little for having eaten my lunch already. Christ, I'm so bored. They could have put a TV in this shoebox. Well, they couldn't if they wanted to close the door, but even so ...

After an hour sitting there counting the parking spaces in view (there are either seventy-six or seventy-seven, if you're interested) I decide to head back over to the complex. I know Fat Paul told me not to leave my post, but I'm hungry and bored. I can't sit in here any longer. It's only when I'm halfway across the car park I realise I've left my wallet at home, for fuck's sake.

It's as I'm just heading back to the Portakabin that a battered, white Transit pulls up to the barrier. Before I've remembered my lines about telling them to fuck off, politely, a huge gorilla in a boiler suit and balaclava jumps out the van and sticks a sawn-off shotgun in my face.

'Get in the fucking van. Try anything and you won't be going home,' Gorilla Man screams in my face. I can only see his teeth and eyes and they both need fucking cleaning.

I mean, is there anything you can say to that? I can't think of anything and just start to climb in. Maybe it's because I'm stoned, but I don't actually feel much fear, I just keep thinking that Gorilla Man needs to clean his teeth in his choice of work, dealing with the public and all. Politeness costs nothing.

The back of the van contains two smaller men, the chimps of the operation I assume. They all wear the same boiler suits and balaclavas, and there's more dust than in my spare room.

'Knock him out, Stan,' Gorilla Man instructs the chimp closest to the front.

'Hang on!' I yell, but it's too late, Stan's already trying and failing to knock me out with the butt of his gun.

'Argh, you fucker, ARGH!' I shout. It's funny, but the more he hits me, and the longer I'm still awake, the more angry I get; I don't so much feel the pain. There's more frustration that I have to be awake throughout this lame attempt by Stan to knock me out. After several whacks I just play dead, it's easier all round.

'Done,' Stan tells everyone.

'You made a fucking meal of that, Stan,' the other chimp says.

'Fuck off, Pete. As if you'd have done any better. It isn't like we've practised techniques for this,' says Stan.

'We fucking will later if you two old cunts don't stop flirting,'

Gorilla Man tells them both from the front. 'Now tie Sleeping Beauty up and don't take too long about it.'

'OK,' the chimps tell him.

The only one I haven't heard speak yet is the driver. I don't, either. He stays silent as the chimps do a better job than expected of tying me up, then they all exit the van, locking it as they go.

Brilliant. A gang of armed criminals have tied me up in the back of a dusty old van on my first night in a new job. And my head is starting to hurt now, too. Makes me wish I'd stayed on the dole. Fucking Job Centre and their insistence on job seekers doing just that.

I struggle a bit and realise I am tied tight. The chimps must have been in the Scouts when everyone else was practising caving their mates' heads in down the boxing club. Even if I do manage to untie a hand, I don't have battery on my phone. Fucking Beach Racer. I just have to lie there.

After what seems like about a week I hear alarms going off all around me and then I hear feet running across the car park. If anything happens, it is going to happen now. The van doors are yanked open and, after I have had what seems like ten or twenty large heavy bags chucked on me, the chimps return.

'We fucking did it!' Gorilla Man shouts as he jumps in the van. There is lots of whooping and celebrating going on as the van skids towards the exit.

'Hang on, what about this one?' Stan asks.

'Sling him in the Portakabin,' Gorilla Man orders. Thank god I am not going to be kept with this lot any longer than necessary.

The van stops and I feel a couple of pairs of hands on me. I'm dragged to the open door and thrown into the Portakabin. Well, halfway in, it isn't big enough for all of me, so my legs are just left outside the door.

It's as I'm just thinking about having a go at getting myself up off the floor that someone enters the Portakabin and a familiar voice says, 'See, I told you it's a varied job,' and I feel something being put into my top pocket. 'You never seen a thing,' he says, and the van drives off.

APT PUPIL

Boozers, I love them. The people, the layout, the décor — everything. Then there's the beer, of course. I fucking LOVE the beer. None of these new age alcoholic milkshakes that the student types who insist on coming to my local drink. Just beer for me.

I hate students. They don't do anything productive. They just sit there staring at the world and nattering to themselves about how great they'll all be one day. It's always 'one day' with this lot. There's just no get up and go in them.

I use my local most days. I ain't an alky or nothing, I just like the atmos. Except when the local adult learners come in to shake each other's satchels in celebration of spelling their name right.

I mean, I work hard six days a week — well four and a half out of seven. Call me a liar if you like, but I contribute more to society than these wasters ever will. The times I'm sat at home catching up when I could be in my local, I tell you; if I got paid for all the overtime, my salary would be doubled, I swear.

I saw one of them pay for three drinks with a cheque the other day. For god's sake! A cheque for under a fiver! Barry, the landlord, made them buy a couple of packets of crisps to make the money up. He hates them as much as I do. Mind you, he still takes their money. If I was him, I wouldn't. If it was down to me I'd ban the lot of the chair-stealing sad acts. In fact, I have actually made a few anonymous signs, but Barry always tells me to take them down, says there is more than one way to skin a toad, whatever the fuck that means. I hope he hasn't tried skinning one without me; I'd like to see that.

'What the fuck does that mean?' I asked Barry one night after he'd rolled out his favourite cliché.

'Well, Greg, I've got a plan to get them lot back for keeping on making my bogs smell of that Wanja leaf,' Barry told me, leaning in closely and lowering his already gravel-like voice.

'Can I put a hate poster up?' I ask hopefully.

'Give it a rest with the posters, will you Greg? You don't even spell them right,' Barry says, a little louder than necessary, making old Tom and big Jimmy Temple piss themselves at the other end of the bar.

'I bloody ...' I start.

'Spastic!' Big Jim hollers, interrupting me mid-denial. Everyone in the pub laughed. Even the fucking students that were over near the pool table. I vowed to remember their public disrespect towards me.

'OK, so no posters. What are you going to do, Bazzer?' I asked, continuing to ignore big Jim who had started making spak noises.

'I think we should do what him next door,' Barry continued, with a flick of his head towards Stavros on the other side of the wall, 'does to everyone's chips, Greg.'

'Spunk in them?'

'Oh god! He don't do that, does he?' Barry asked, repulsed.

'I wouldn't put it past him, the filthy bastard. I haven't been in since I saw him sweating into the fryer. Smiling away he was. He must have known he was leaking into my dinner.'

'The dirty bastard! That's the last time I eat there,' Barry spat out in disgust.

'Yeah, don't eat there, mate. So, what's the plan to get the students?'

'Well, I was thinking about spiking the bastards with Kaliber and then letting them pretend to be drunk. But I might use Stavros's trick now and just gob in their drink.'

'Erggrrrrh,' Jim shouts out.

'Quiet, Jim,' Barry tells him, waving his shushing finger about and giving the students a sideways glance.

'You could gob in their Kaliber,' I offer hopefully.

'That's a grand idea. I must ask you though, Greg, why do you hate them so much? I mean, they're your students ...'

PETE SORTWELL

ONE FLEW OVER THE POLICEMAN'S BONNET

The doctors had been telling me for ages I was 'stressed', then I had what they called a 'psychotic delusional breakdown'. That's bollocks, though. I saw it as a break *through*, as this was when I became aware of my calling in life – my one chance to do something good for the world and, more particularly, my wife, Mary. *They* didn't see it like that though: *they* locked me up. I know how Jesus felt – betrayed!

I'd never really given karma too much thought before I went into hospital. In my job it can be hard to think about any kind of spiritual stuff – all the scumbags I've nicked made me see things black and white, right and wrong. I never even considered the science behind it until God spoke to me and filled me in on a few things. The role God and His angels have in making sure all is even in the world is huge. It is too much for the normal human brain.

My mission is to kill a mugger. Doing it will level things out and make sure that me and Mary are safe in retirement, which is fast approaching. I've been an exceptional copper over the years, arresting thousands of lowlifes, probably the reason God chose me as one of his Karma Agents.

The mistake I made was telling people what I know: the knowledge I was given is too much for the normal man to comprehend.

I thought people would understand. It isn't like they know everything and every outcome of all the ways of the world, is it? No. They just think they do.

But I really do.

'For your own safety, Fred,' they'd said.

'You'll be out in no time,' they'd said.

Mary said I would feel better and understand things when I had given my head a holiday.

Eight weeks they kept me in. Locking me up didn't stop me getting my messages from God, though, He sends them in loads of ways: T-shirt slogans, the TV and the radio. No one can stop them coming, not even the liquid cosh they put in me. I refused the tablets, but several burly 'nurses' jumped me and injected it. Knelt on my head and everything. I'm told these are Devil's agents hell bent on destroying my mission. I need to watch out for these.

My mate, Mike, wants me to stay on sick leave then retire when the time comes. I have other ideas, though. I WILL be donning my uniform one last time.

I got a message through the TV pointing out Simon, a hopeless drug addict and a thief. He used to nick cheese exclusively, but things changed when his parents – nice, good people – cut him off after he was booted out of St Paul's Rehab for dealing. He's been given every chance to sort himself out and hasn't. He now mugs old people to get his fix.

I'd been walking one day thinking over the message about Simon when I saw a T-shirt slogan. It told me: *Just do it.* And I knew there was no mistake, no mix up. Simon has to die.

Today is the day it is going to happen.

***

'Morning, love, alright?' Mary asks as I come back in from the shed.

'Good, ta, love; you?' I reply. I've been out checking my uniform and badge are still where I left them. I keep that to myself. She doesn't know, doesn't need to.

'Yeah, I'm fine. Have you remembered I'm off to the library, then meeting Karen for coffee? I'll see you after lunch. Remember Mike is coming at one,' Mary reminds me.

'I have. Have fun, I'm going to clear the shed out,' I say, kissing her on the cheek.

'OK, ta-ta, love you,' Mary says, taking her coat off the peg.

'Love you, too,' I say, watching her leave.

As soon as she gets in the street I think I see her on her mobile. Who would she be calling?

Stop worrying, Fred, she is not clever enough to have worked anything out. No one is clever like you, God tells me. *Plenty of time.*

Ten minutes later, having allowed time for her to return if she's forgotten something, I head to the shed to put on my uniform for the last time.

***

It feels good walking down the path wearing my uniform again, powerful. Not as powerful as I feel with the knowledge that I can speak to and hear God. I mean it must be Him that is talking to me through the TV and giving me all these signs. I have thought about it a lot and this is the only logical explanation. I've done too much good for it to be anyone else.

I'd have taken the car if it hadn't been hidden from me, so I have to walk. Luckily the estate I am heading to is only ten minutes away. I should move, really, but then again I shouldn't have to. This is why God has come to me and given me these instructions. He doesn't think it is fair, either.

As I am walking I feel elated. I buzz from knowing I have been chosen. Some of the mad people in the hospital tried to tell me they had been given missions, too, but they were all fucking bonkers and didn't make sense. I saw through them straight away. Some were agents of the Devil placed there only there to hinder my work, some were just plain, honest-to-God nutters.

I think about how clever I have been, tricking all the shrinks into thinking that they were good at their jobs. This is just one more pointer to the fact I am working for a higher being than these losers. I doubt they even know I was spitting my meds out. Even if I didn't, the messages kept coming. They just made me feel too muddled.

I know what I need to do and nothing is going to stop me.

I also think about how I am going to do the job. I have got my keys on me with the penknife attached – the little lock knife I used to use in the Scouts – along with the second police baton I nicked a couple of years ago. I took it just in case. I wasn't being given messages then, but I must have known this day would come, so I just didn't give it in one day and nothing was ever said. This is the thing about the police, nothing is as tight or organised as we are led to believe.

I have not been told how to finish the job yet. I suppose the less people that know, the better. Maybe I am being given license to do as I wish. I'll know when I look into the scumbag's pinned eyes. If I am allowed to do as I wish, I'll make the bastard suffer as much as possible.

It doesn't take me long to get to the Granbyhill Estate. I know which number Simon lives in, I have been there often enough. The time is 10.55. I shouldn't think it will be long before he is up and about. I choose to wait in the underpass.

A couple of local yobs ride past on their stolen, hand-repainted bikes and make a few pig noises, but I give them a bit of the old crazy eyes and ask them to come over to me and repeat it and they fuck off.

As they go one of them is pointing to his body and then back to me, I think he clocked I have no stab vest on.

Someone walks past in a T-shirt that says *Relax;* there's some other writing, but only the one word sticks out. That's a message, things are still on track, everything is going as it should.

I was wrong. I have to wait another half hour, but I keep myself concealed and busy myself thinking about the future.

Then it happens: I see the sorry piece of shit in the distance heading out of his block, dirty and scruffy as he always his. My mobile has rung a couple of times – Mike, probably checking that I'll be in when he gets there. I haven't answered it, though.

As Simon gets to the underpass and sees me, I see him hesitate. It must be the uniform that scares the piece of shit. If I were an old lady he'd have run towards me, eyes wide with excitement.

I stand my ground, eyeing him as he walks towards me. As he gets closer to the middle of the underpass I move towards him; he is getting edgy now.

'What?' he says, almost shitting his knickers. I can only assume this is because he's scared of getting nicked before he gets his fix for the day. Well, he won't need that shit where he's going. If I knew more about it I would try and injure him fatally AND make sure he has to go through withdrawal. I don't, though, and the only message I have got through so far is to finish him.

'Come here, son,' I say in a menacing tone. And the thick twat does.

'What do you want? I'm busy,' he tells me matter of factly.

'Come here, I need to talk to you,' I say, as he moves closer and closer.

With each step he takes I keep hearing the same thing.

Do him, save Mary, do him, save Mary. Like a tape on repeat.

I reach round to get my baton; his legs are going to be first.

'Hang on a minute,' he says, just an arm's length away.

WHACK!

I crack him on the side of the knee and he's down before he knows what's happened.

This is it, the moment I have been building up to for months, the moment that was nearly taken from me by the Judases in my life.

'Argh, what you do that for?' Simon whimpers from his face down position on the ground.

'Turn over!' I scream. 'You mugging scumbag, you ain't going to harm my Mary now. TURN OVER!'

'What the fu—' he is saying, but I stop that with another belt to the kidneys. I know that hurt.

'Argh!'

'I said, turn over.' I want to see the fear. The fear he has caused so many will now be coming back on him tenfold. This is good, better than expected.

He's going in the water once I've caved his head in, to double check that the bastard is dead.

As he turns, I see his eyes: the fear is there, I can see it.

Doof! He kicks me in the balls – hard. Before I can react and whack him again he has slid out from under me, he's up and he puts the boot into my ribs, knocking the wind out of me. I'm down. *Shit, he's getting away. I need a message.*

Fighting for breath and ignoring the infernal pain from my bollocks, I try and tune in to what's coming through the channels. Then it comes: *Get up and get after him. Time's running out!*

I'm up and after him as soon as I can catch a breath; the fucker has a head start, though. He is up the embankment and across the road before I am at the end of the bridge. I didn't think a fuck-up like him would be as quick. Maybe his survival instinct has kicked in.

I cannot lose him – EVERYTHING depends on this!

Getting to the road, I see Simon jumping on a bus. That is far too public. I can't finish him there. The message comes and it's a good un: I stand in front of the next car to come round the corner. As I stand there, I worry a little that it won't stop, then I remember: I am looked after, it just won't happen.

'Hello, Officer, what can I do for you?' the old dear in the car says. Typical – I am commandeering the car of Miss Daisy.

'Car! I need your car, there's a criminal on the loose!'

'But, but, I—' I don't wait for her to finish and I help her out the rest of the way, well, drag her. Wrong, but God won't mind as I am on His mission.

I'm in the car and after the bus like a shot, leaving the driver in the road wondering if her day can get much worse.

After couple of hairy overtakes I am behind the bus. I've got to get him fast or Mary will be home and see I'm not there.

After three little stops the bus waits to get into Greyfriars' stop, which has a few lanes for buses. I know he'll get off here, me and Mary do all the time, you have to change here to get into town.

The radio's on in the car. I hadn't noticed up till now, but as the message comes through I suddenly tune in to it: I hear *You gotta roll with it, don't let anybody stand in your way*. And I know how to finish the job.

As the bus pulls into the stop I hang back a bit, I need a run up to finish the job. There's a bit of a crowd and for a moment I worry about the other people there, but they'll move; he has a knackered leg, he won't be able to. I hear *You gotta roll with it* again and I know that I'm right – the power will move the others for me.

Suddenly I have to stop thinking, as there he is.

With as much wheel spin as I can get out of a Fiat Punto, I bomb towards him. I mount the kerb, the crowd scatters, and Simon stands directly in front of me, right in my line of fire.

Just as I am about to hit him, someone runs from the bus and pushes Simon out of the way. I collide with the person that does and they fly over the bonnet. As I look in the mirror, I see Mary's distinctive coat roll off the roof and on to the ground.

PETE SORTWELL

WIN-WIN

I'm sat in this fucking probation waiting room again. I seem to spend half my life sat waiting for Judith.

'Just take a seat, Simon,' says the receptionist, 'Judith will be out in a moment.' Fucking lying bitch.

Every bloody week it's the same. Now I have to sit here next to this middle-aged bald man who is trying to justify his sexual perversions.

'I swear she looked sixteen ...' he starts to say.

'Look, Noncey, I may look and smell like I ain't washed in a week, but I am NOT one of your lot! If you don't fuck off with your kiddie fiddling bullshit, I am going to put my boot in your balls, CCTV or not. OK!' I tell him, deciding not to beat around the bush.

'Err, err I was just ...' he starts.

'Shuuut it,' I snarl, which he does.

We sit in relative silence until he starts sniffling, attracting the attention of the receptionist. The bitch gives me the evil eye and picks up the phone. I'm a petty shoplifter, not a sexual deviant like him. He hurts kids and I'm the one judged for making him cry? I hate it here. Why should he get a chair, and a coffee, and the right to sit next to me? The only chair he should get is an electric one.

Hang on a minute! Where's my fucking coffee?

Behind the door leading to the interview rooms, someone curses and it sounds as if they have dropped some files. 'Oh, damn and blast!' The muffled voice is Judith. I prepare to stand and smile as she opens the door, holding a folder and loads of paperwork, all crumpled up. She doesn't even look at me. 'Brian, come through, please,' she says, and old Noncey Bri stands up and greets her.

'Hang on. I had an appointment ten minutes ago,' I protest.

'Yes. Well. I'm running behind today. *You* will just have to wait,' she replies.

'Oh, for fuck's sake!' I say.

'I heard that, Simon.' Judith informs me in a tone I know so well.

'Well, I didn't say it in sign language,' I reply, in my pissed off sarky voice. I've been waiting to say that for ages and I feel quite proud of myself for slipping it in. Shame no one is around to hear it except for Noncie and Judas.

'Anymore of your abusive behaviour to me, the staff or other clients, and I will have you removed from here and you WILL be breached Simon,' Judas tells me, no doubt making herself feel a little more powerful than she looks walking off into the sunset with a paedo.

I opt for wobbling my head from side to side and mouthing what she has just said by way of reply.

I'm left for a few moments to regret not saving my great joke for when someone else was round to hear it, but I am not alone for long. A couple of young chavs bowl in, throwing about the 'init bruv seen seen's' Those chav twats are forever giving me shit. These two poor excuses for tracksuit enthusiasts are from my estate and immediately they turn their attention disorders towards me.

'Si, Si, what up, son?' the one with his own name tattooed on his arm says.

Son? I ain't your fucking son, mate! I fingered your mum at school, I think to myself. 'Hello Mickey,' I say.

'What the Fed's got you for this time? I know it ain't no kiddie porn, you can't afford a pooter, innit ha-ha,' he says, earning himself some knuckle love from his mate, Trevor. From what I can see, Trevor is lucky to even see me with the way his eyes point. He's ginger, too, and a future serial killer if ever I saw one.

'Nicking,' I reply, keeping my eyes away from the evil ginger. It's hard when you can't tell where they're looking. I opt to stare at the wall.

'Seen, seen. What you get away with?' Mickey asks me.

'I don't wanna talk about it'.

'Oh. My. Days,' Mickey says, forgetting he is not, and never has been, black. 'You got busted nicking cheese again, didn't you!? Oh, you retard! When will you learn, you fucking crack 'ed?'

'No, it wasn't cheese, actually,' I lie.

Come on, Judith, you twat bag, don't leave me sitting here. I wish I had a coffee so I could throw it all over my own crotch just to take the attention away from my nicking.

'Ah, Trev, this joker gets caught nicking cheese every other week,' Mickey needlessly tells Trevor, which prompts Trevor to start to talk to the poster to my far right.

'You wanna buy some puff, grade A?'

I look round to see if the poster's interested, then realise it's me he's talking to rather than the poster or his own nose.

'Weed is much better than that shit you're on,' he continues, regardless.

I must be sat in his blind spot or something.

'We're sat in probation with grasses everywhere,' I say, nodding at the receptionist who is taking notes while trying to make it look like she is writing a really important date in the dairy or something. This is why she's a receptionist in a place that crap criminals are already in, rather than Secret Sheila of MI5.

'Ah, dese fools can't touch a brudda,' Trevor tells me and his nose, which brings on some more brudda love in the form of some 'street' hand holding from Mickey.

'I'll think about it,' I reply, then decide to wander outside for a quick butt rollie I made earlier from the contents of the handy ash tray outside the door. Thankfully the pair of nipples in hoods stay indoors and discuss ways to get crisis loans. 'I told them I washed my money last week, bruv, innit, got sixty quid, ha ha,' I hear Mickey lying as I leave.

As I come back in, the bredjins have gone. For fuck's sake, their appointments were before me too.

I sit and wait for my son-of-a-bitch probation officer. After half an hour of trying to will Judith dead using only my mind, Peter the pervert bounds in wearing shorter than short shiny shorts and a puffer jacket.

'Christ, they're all in today,' I say, hoping he'll hear me, get offended, and start screaming and punching himself like he does. He doesn't like being made fun of, or being called Peter the Pervert, but how can someone be sensitive to jibes when they pull their socks up that far and wear Clarks shoes?

'I have an appointment with my offending rehabilitation assistant,' Peter says, all-matter-of-fact, to the reception lady.

'OK, Peter, I'll call Dave down now,' she replies, with a smile she only extends to men in headbands, it seems.

'Thank you, Barbara,' Peter says, teaching me something new. After two months of coming here, I've finally learned her name. I promise myself an extra bag later to help me forget it again, just so I don't slip and call her it. I don't want to give her any idea that I might like her. I don't. I fucking hate her. I hate them all.

'No problem, Peter. How is your mother?' Barbara ... err ... shit ... I mean nameless-woman-that-I-hate, enquires.

'Fucking embarrassed, I should think,' I say, this time hitting the target just shy of bullseye.

'Fuck off! Fuck off FUUUUCK OFFFFF!' Peter shouts at me while rocking forwards and backwards in the way that spakos do.

'Steady on, Petey. There's no need to make a song and dance about things,' I say, impressing myself for the second time today. It only annoys him further and he starts to grind his teeth. It's loud enough to hear, but his mouth isn't moving. He's staring at me too, like ... well, like a madman.

Peter is not really a pervert. He just looks like one due to the way he dresses and the odd way he acts. That pretty much ticks the boxes in my mind, and that of every other small-minded crim. We all need someone weaker, uglier and stranger to look down on.

Peter soon goes through to the consulting rooms. I'm still waiting.

Jed comes in, he's someone I know from the 'wet zone,' which is basically a bus stop round the side of the pound shop on the edge of town where we're allowed to drink. He's always there; he likes a good drink. Doesn't touch the gear, though, just his drink, and a meth script from Boots once a morning.

'PerrrrrrVVVEEeerrrt,' Jed shouts out, like a boxing compere, as soon as he spots Peter's back end going through the door.

'Fuck you, boy, you fucking boy!' Peter shouts from the other side of the door as it clicks shut. There is then an almighty bang, bang, bang on the door followed by a deafening alarm. The sound scares the shit out of me – Jed and I cover our ears. Jed allows his left ear one more second of pain as he takes his finger out, to breath on his finger nails and rub them on his right tit, in celebration. Smiling, he comes over and sits next to me, raising his eyes and putting his fingers firmly in his ears. The alarm stops after two minutes and from the other side of the door it sounds like Peter is fighting half of the probation service single-handed.

'Get off me you cuuuuunts!' Peter's muffled voice screams, and a dozen shouts of 'calm down' follow this.

'Fucking hell, hold his legs, he's just kneed me,' someone shouts out. After a few more bangs the noise stops, as Peter is dragged off.

'Sad, really, when you think about it, isn't it?' Jed says, with a smile.

'Ha ha, yeah, but fucking funny,' I reply.

'Yeah,' Jed chuckles.

I decide to try my luck and ask Jed for a smoke. 'You got any smokes, Jed?' I ask.

'Yeah, here y'are,' Jed says, opening a twenty pack of tailor mades.

'Ta, mate,' I say, as I take one. I know what the plan for the rest of the day is. It's clearly giro day for Jed, and if I can't manipulate him into giving me some of his giro money, I'll take it when he's not looking or too pissed to fight me off. I mean, he's a mate, I suppose, but who cares about that when it comes to free money? It'd mean I won't have to nick cheese, whole racks of batteries or A-Z's out of Waterstone's, then sell them to the corner shops. The bottom line is, he's got it and I want it. This means I'll get it. We head outside as I ask him what his plans for the day are.

'Well,' he muses. 'Could get pissed, I suppose?' Like this was ever not going to happen anyway. 'You fancy it, Si?' Jed asks.

'Gotta do some graft first, mate,' I say, pulling on the first of many of Jed's Lamberts.

'Oh, you ain't are you?' he whines. 'I ain't coming with you again, I got coming here for three months as a reward last time.'

'I gotta, mate. I'll be sick else,' I say, laying it on thick.

I'm angling for half his meth; he gets double what he needs, if not more, to keep the wolf from the door every day. He normally swaps it for a drink or some blueys, but today he is the king in the *king for a day, cunt for a fortnight* giro cycle.

'I suppose I could give you my excess if you sort us a frosty shat in the week.'

'Oh, that's a lovely offer mate, are you sure? I'd still need to get a few bits for the voddy, but not a lot,' I reply.

'Don't worry about that. I'll get you drink,' he offers kindly. Mug.

'Just return the favour,' he says, adding a condition I have no intention of keeping.

'Yeah, course, mate, course,' I assure Jed in my best sincere voice.

We flick the fags over the edge of the rail, bouncing them off the nearest car bonnet, and go back inside just as Noncey is being shown out by Judith. I don't sit down, expecting her to call me through, but she turns on her heels and heads back towards the door.

'Hey! Ain't we having this fucking appointment?' I shout after her.

'Simon, that's three people you have verbally abused since being here. I'm going to ask you to leave and mark you down as a breach for non-attendance,' she says.

'Huh?' I say. 'You mean I don't have to come?'

'I'm not seeing you today, no,' she replies.

'And it's for verbal abuse?' I ask, hoping.

'Yes.'

'Oh. Well, I might as well make it worth it then ... You fucking shit cunt ugly fuck. Ya saggy titted bitch,' I shout, as she walks through the door.

I turn to Jed and shrug with a smile. 'Right, I'm off down Tesco. I'll meet you back here in an hour,' I say.

As I'm walking towards town I feel like a winner. I've not had to sit with that bitch and I've got a free day on the wreck out of Jed. Mind you, Judith is no doubt thinking the same, she has got out of sitting in a room with my smelly arse and she has got to punish me for it too.

A real win-win situation.

INSIDE I'M DANCING

Every day I'd sit in the same spot. They all ignored me or talked over or at me.

I remember one of them heading over to patronise me.

'Oh, Ricky, you look thirsty.' My face hadn't changed all day.

She forced a drink into my mouth. I didn't really want it, but took the nip of the adult cup anyway. Well, what choice did I have? It was a case of drink it or wear it.

Nothing really changed, day in, day out. I sat in the same boring old place, had the same awful people getting in my face and treating me like dirt.

When I was three weeks old, my mum threw me against the wall and all I was left with was the ability to think, learn stuff and move my arms about five inches. My body hardly works at all, but my head is normal, I think. It's not good enough to control my body, but it can remember most things.

No one there knew about my brain being OK, they didn't bother with tests. It had been the same for years. I worked out a blinking system with an old teacher, but she died and that lot never bothered to read any files of mine. I was money to them and that was that.

The people who worked there all claimed to be Christian. That's rubbish, I listened to a talking Bible once and nowhere did it say treat people with less ability than you with contempt, from what I heard it told people to be nice to others and love thy neighbour. Those people never showed me or the other residents any love or tolerance. Although they were happy to drag us all to the church to meet their friends under the guise of 'religious commitments'. The boss was happy for them to go and she was there too, making herself look all great wheeling us lot in and letting her friends 'heal' us, which basically was a practice that involved a large amount of people touching us. It made me feel dirty to have a lot of people grabbing at me, chanting.

I've been hit, starved, left in dirty, wet pads for hours, had food left in my hair for a week after I've sneezed when being fed. The worst part was at night, they put me to bed at 8 p.m. every night. I was left with no music, no talking books or TV. I didn't need much sleep — I did nothing most days but sit waiting for someone to rescue me. I never really went anywhere else. I got pushed around the park sometimes, but not often, only normally when one of the workers needed a fag or to make a lengthy personal phone call. The things I heard discussed! They were all bad people and seemed to be criminals through and through. From passport fraud to selling drugs, I don't think I went on a walk without hearing about some scam or another. The guy that used to hit me seemed to really believe that he could beat the need to use the toilet out of me. I'd get digs in the ribs and on the top and back of my head, it happened so much I got used to it. The guy didn't even try to hide it, why would he? No one cared if I was hurt, upset or abused in front of them. It was normal life in that place.

I thought about my mum a lot during the night. It was when I felt most alone. Sometimes I'd wonder if I'd done something wrong, if I was different to all the other babies. Other mums didn't throw their babies into the wall. Maybe I was a loud crier. She'd probably had enough of me. I got fed up of Ashley, my house mate, screaming sometimes.

Mum's a beautiful lady. The last time I saw her was a few months ago on my twenty-first birthday, she visited and brought me a big silver tankard with my name on. She talked to me like a person. It was nice, but the lady with her took her away again, she always takes her away. Mum did kiss me when she left, that was nice.

Sometimes I tried to remember and replicate her soft kiss on the side of my face. It was hard, though, as I'd lose concentration easily. But it kept me going at night time – thinking about her.

When there was a new member of staff starting work, the owner, Felicity, used to explain my history to them across the lounge in front of everyone. She really made my mother sound bad and didn't mind saying that she'd ban her if it was her choice. She kept saying that my mother was sick, that she was the devil incarnate. I used to have a teddy that smelt like Mum, she bought me it. However, it was taken from my room and never returned. I cried for a long time about that. They just thought I had a cold, though. No one cared that I was upset. They never did.

I've been on holiday to Morocco with the staff, the owner of the home is from there. Every year we're all paraded in front of the family and local townsfolk to show them how well she's done for herself and how kind she is. I got really bad sunburn on one of those holidays. It didn't stop her dragging us round the town to various family members' houses every day of the trip and leaving me out in the heat, though. I was sick over myself one day. When I was being pushed back to the van, I was told angrily that I was an embarrassment and that god wouldn't forgive me. I didn't care, though, I took it as a little victory. I tried to get them when I could. I wouldn't have done that in the home, though – they'd have left me covered in it, as they'd left me in my own filth on many an occasion, overnight mostly. When I'd get put to bed I'd hear one say to the other, between the two it took to lift me, that I stank; they'd always choose to leave me till the morning, though.

The residents had to pay for the holiday. I don't know how much got paid to them every week to look after me, but I know that all the money paid into my bank was saved up, along with the other residents' money, and used to buy the flights for the trip: ours and the staff's. While it was being saved up, I was left to wear secondhand clothes and eat the cheapest food going, all in the same stripy Tesco packaging.

There's so much more, but I'm tired, can we finish tomorrow?

'That's more than enough for today, Mr Robinson, thank you,' the detective said. He stood up to leave. 'It's a great bit of kit, that computer, isn't it?' he said to my new nurse on the way out.

BOOK SAMPLES

PETE SORTWELL

THE VILLAGE IDIOT REVIEWS

Read the first three reviews from the book:

New 3 Pants Pack Men's Classic 100% Cotton Y Style Briefs To Fit Sizes Small Medium Large X-Large 2X-Large

A sturdy hold, but I think there was something up with the material.

Living alone, I need to keep a substantial number of Y-fronts at any one time. This is due to how far away my mother lives away and not owning a washing machine myself. A couple of these three packs were perfect for my needs.

I must say as I pulled on a fresh pair on the day of delivery, I instantly noticed how supporting they were of little Frank and his two pet bulldogs. They were a very soft feel and made me feel all warm and tingly. Not like some pairs I've owned that made poor Frank feel like he was being kettled during a peaceful protest turned bad.

All was well until I paid a visit to the local funfair. Now, I can't blame the full unpleasantness of the ghost train on the pants, or in fact any of it. They shouldn't allow people to go on alone if they're going to have such scary things in there. I think it was when the carnival fellow jumped out and licked my face that I fouled myself in the most horrendously loose and smelly manner. I feel they should also have stricter control on the food hygiene at these traveling funfairs. The smell that presented itself to my new pants was distinctly similar to the three hotdogs I'd consumed shortly before embarking on the journey of dread (as I've come to call it).

What happened next was even more unfortunate; the rugged fair owner had to close the ride for cleansing and publicly told everyone in attendance it was my fault. Due to having soggy pants, I was unable to flee, as I normally would; this resulted in me being cornered between the bearded woman booth and the hook-a-duck stand. I had to be removed by the police for my own safety.

By the time I'd explained that I wasn't, as the crowd called me, a dirty tramp, I was, in fact, someone who had accidently filled his pants due to the above reasons, some of the recycled hotdogs had started to dry, down the back of the legs mainly but some within the pants also.

As luck would have it I was visiting my mother a few days later and was able to get the pants in a hot wash much faster than I normally manage.

Sadly the pair I was wearing the night of the funfair seemed to have stained, and in some places, glued themselves together. They are, for all intents and purposes, ruined, although I have taken the suggestion from Mother to use the soiled pair to polish my bicycle and a sterling job they are doing, too.

My advice: if you're going to visit the funfair wearing these pants, double bag, don't go on the ghost train, and for God's sake, don't eat the hotdogs. The police might not be so quick to act in your area.

-Brian

T&G Woodware Farmyard Crazy Sidney the Sheep Teacosy

Great cosy, but not so great for wearing.

Being a vicar for a small parish in the south of England, I am expected to hold a fair amount of tea parties and get-togethers for my flock, which is invariably the older ladies of the community. Normally I am gracious enough to allow them to make me a woollen tea cosy. These have been, over the years, of mostly good quality, except the time Ethel Morrison presented one to me she'd managed to fashion together out of her husband's incontinence pads, although we've since agreed not to talk about that. However nice the gifts of knitted tea cosies are, once a year I am visited by the bishop, Desmond. He's a jolly old fellow most of the time, although he has been known to get a little bit on the excited side when around new brides. I think it's something to do with the white dresses. Anyway, last month he was due on his annual visit so I needed something a little more sophisticated. Along with tea parties I also run a youth group for the three local children. Denny, the oldest of the gang, introduced me to the internet and the wide range of everything available. Denny also pointed out this sheep-styled cosy and what with there being sheep kept in the paddock next to the rectory, I decided this was a good choice. I just knew Bishop Desmond would be suitably impressed.

I was amazed at how quick the cosy arrived. We ordered at 3 a.m. one morning and it was with us by 10 a.m. the next day. Denny said he thought it would double as a hat and on inspection I have to say I agreed; it *would* bring a smile to Bishop Desmond's face. Things didn't go quite to plan, though. I'd planned to present myself wearing the tea cosy at dinner, an hour or two after serving the first cup of tea to my guests. I had an Irish coffee myself ... well, several. As I was outside the room preparing myself to surprise Bishop Desmond, Millie Wainwright started to choke on the broiled pheasant I'd spent all the morning, and some of the previous evening preparing. Needless to say, me busting into the room wearing a tea cosy didn't raise the mood half as much as I'd hoped. In fact, it raised the anger of Bishop Desmond, who at the time had just finished carrying out the Heimlich manoeuvre on Millie.

In finishing, I'd say leave the cosy on the teapot and leave the jokes to the younger people of your parish.

Denny seemed to find the whole event most amusing.

-Father Frederick

Jesus Fancy Dress Costume Robe, Wig & Beard — One Size

Superior robes.

The youth group fancy dress party was held last week. Father Frederick only had one rule: the people we dress as must come from the Bible. I didn't buy this item as I couldn't get my hands on Father Frederick's credit card for long enough. I did copy it, though. I used a wig I found in the lost property at the church, one of the altar boy outfits that Father Frederick keeps trying to make me wear at this house, and I nabbed a red piece of felt from the church. (I think they use it to rest the collection plates on.) The sandals I had to steal from one of the other kids, Bobby. I think I pulled off the copy well. Once I'd finished I looked very much like Jesus.

It was a great disguise. And with an added bum bag I was able to nick no end of the vicar's stuff. Getting it into my room at the children's home was easy, too, as they didn't think to look in my robes, they were just happy I'd stopped swearing at them instead of talking to them when I came in. For the first few weeks I'd just wafted past them holding up the Vs instead of talking to them. They're still knobs but at least I can get away with stuff if I don't attract negative attention.

If you can afford this outfit, buy it. If not the picture is fantastic to work from.

-Denny

THE OFFICE IDIOT REVIEWS

Read the first three reviews from the book:

Ronhill Men's Advanced Racer Shorts

Almost too short.

Norman Hogsbottom, the man, the boss, the supplier of plugs, is what the sign on my desk states. That's right, I sell plugs. However, being all of these things doesn't mean a man doesn't need to stay fit. I bought these running shorts after seeing the London marathon on TV. I found myself telling the office junior, Sandy, that I had already signed up and been accepted for next year's. I'm not sure what I was thinking; at the time I'd not run since I was at boarding school during shower time with

Dirty McWandery hands, the games teacher.

These shorts seem to be what all the runners wear so I bought a pair. The date was set, I was going to go running one evening after everyone had gone home. I brought a honey sandwich from home for energy. I read that honey is good for that. Well, actually I read that bananas were good, but I don't really like them. I like honey though, so that was what was in the sandwich.

Once all my employees had left I changed into my shorts and navy singlet, wolfed down the honey sandwich, strapped on my Hi-Tec silver running shoes and headed out into the summer night.

I did fairly well, making it across the road and onto the tow path, only resting when walking down the stairway to it, then I headed off again. The lack of air poleaxed me about thirty seconds after that. Checking my watch I saw I'd been out the office for four minutes, which is embarrassing by anyone's standards. I decided it would be a good idea to walk and even ignored the taunts of 'Jimmy Savile' from the kids on the other side of the canal.

As I was walking, that's when it happened. All of a sudden I felt this stinging, burning pain on my pee-pee. It must have slipped out. The pain was worse than when I caught an STD in the navy. I thought I'd been shot for a second, then felt the wasp flying about in my shorts. Started thumping at my shorts trying to get the wasp out. This caused me some discomfort but it was the kind that gets worse over time, so when I was violently hitting myself in the groin area I wasn't feeling the physical pain of anything other than the wasp sting. The punching didn't seem to work so I went for the grabbing method; however, that did bring on instant tennis ball pain. The pain was starting to affect my balance, I was going light-headed in the way I have done before when I've fainted. Try as I might, I just couldn't get the wasp out. I began to panic. I could hear the kids laughing from the other side and I think I finally managed to get the wasp out before I slipped and toppled into the canal. That brought me to from the pain coma I seemed to have slipped into. Scrambling out, I'm sure I clambered over a dead sheep. It was the worst experience of my life.

I think it is partly to do with how short these shorts are and partly because I'm a messy eater when it comes to honey sandwiches.

My advice if you buy these shorts: if you're using them for running and not just sitting about the office (which is what I use them for now) then don't eat honey sandwiches in a messy fashion before you go out. The shorts are just too short. There is no way you can avoid any honey falling onto your pee-pee. Well, that's my experience, anyway.

Three stars as they are comfortable.

-Mr Hogsbottom

15 White Paper Carrier Bags Party Bags

Great for carrying tall turds.

These are great. The handles are fantastic, as when you're carrying one containing tall items, such as baguettes, they can poke out of the corner and not touch any skin. Unfortunately I had to carry something far more sinister than bread-based snacks.

There's always a mess to clean up in the toilet. I know, toilets are *meant* to be dirty but the evil that lurks in the toilets where I work is like something out of a horror movie.

The other day I went in to attend to my cleaning duties and there was a log so big not even the business end of the steel brush would break it down. There was no way it was making it round the U-bend. It was stood up straight. I couldn't see any paper in the bowl either, so either it had been a clean break or it'd managed to stay prone during the flush. I soon discovered it was the latter as it wouldn't move when I flushed several times either. Seriously, it must have been painful for the person who put it there. Still, it being my job, I started the task of breaking it down with the toilet brush, although we already know how that worked out.

In the end I had to fish it out. It was the last resort, but after trying and failing to break it down with bleach there was nothing else I could think of. I'd been for lunch while the bleach took effect so had my newly vacant sandwich bag with me in order to contain the beast. I didn't have any gloves, so I used my trusty pliers to pick the gigantic turd up. The plan was to take it out the car park and sling it over the hedge.

As well as being huge, this thing also stunk to high heaven, too. It was dreadful and the faster I walked the more wind I generated, and the down force created forced the odour up my nostrils harder, although I didn't really equate the two things at the time, I just wanted it out of my office and out of my hands as quickly as possible. I think it was the bleach that finally made me faint. I'd forgotten I'd soaked it with the stuff. Thinking back, I know I should have sprayed it down with a flush or at least rinsed it under the tap; alas, I didn't and suffered the consequences. Those consequences mainly involving fainting on the back stairs then, when I woke up, rubbing my face with the hand that was still clutching King Kong's finger. It was the smell that woke me up. It was worse than any wake up call I've ever had. I thought I was in bed at home for a second. Although once I realised that I hadn't had a dirty bed accident the reality was even worse.

Now, I'm the cleaner, I knew I'd have to clean it up in the end — if it wasn't me, I'd have left it there for someone else to deal with, but I'd only have been summoned to deal with it once it was discovered. So, still feeling fairly light-headed, I picked myself up and carried on with my task. It was when I got outside that I realised the package had snapped. I'd had enough, though, and just got in the car and drove home after slinging the remaining half.

Unfortunately the offender has dropped the dirty bomb three more times since then, so I've ordered these. The handles make it easier to dispose of. I get a good bit of purchase behind my swing using them.

-John the cleaner

Adios Max Maximum Strength Weight Loss Tablets — 100 Tablets

These won't make you sleep with the office ginger.

It is so dull in the office I work in. The boss, Mr Hogsbottom, is a posh boy who is as thick as a tin of soup. I have very little, other than ordering the boss's dinner and filling out a few forms, to do. I spend my time eating, it's nice to have a treat every now and then. Although, of course, this brings troubles of its own. I'm overweight. There, I said it. I'm a big fat bird.

I ordered these to try and help. I thought Amazon would be a better place to buy from as the ones I brought from a Chinese website did some strange things to me. I didn't want to eat at all, that was the good part, but I was sweating, erratic and wide awake all the time. My husband said they were like speed, although I've never taken drugs so don't know if that's true or not. All I know is those pills put me in a place I liked, to a point. The downside, other than the sweating, which as a fat person, I'm used to anyway, was that I liked everyone a lot more than I normally do. That and the increased libido. I was horny ALL the time. Which when you work in an office is no good, there is only so many times you can hide in the toilet trying to scratch that itch.

I'm ashamed to say, I ended up sleeping with Mark, the idiot health and safety officer. Well, we didn't even sleep, just met up behind the factory a few times. Every day. For a week. I think it was his breath repeating on me on the way home that made me realise something wasn't quiet right. I normally hate him. When I was on the Chinese pills though, I liked him immensely. I flushed the pills the Sunday after my week of passion with Mark and ordered these. I'm relieved to say that they've restored my sanity to normal and I was able to sneer at Mark with all my usual gusto when he tipped me the wink around half ten on the first day without my old diet pills. He got the message. It makes me shudder to think about now, though. There was a side effect to those other pills too. I had a hallucination. Just one. A giant fish outside the window, just swimming about. It was so real I didn't know I'd been seeing things until I sat down and thought about it. I mean huge goldfish don't fly about near second floor office windows, do they?

I've not seen as big a difference in the weight with these new pills yet. I'm hoping that they will kick in. My appetite has come back big time after my week of not really eating at all.

I'm not expecting the weight loss I got from the other pills, but some would be nice.

The other positive thing about these pills is that I'm not finding myself dancing to any music. Least of all classical FM, which is what we're forced to listen to in the office. I was getting strange looks doing 'big fish, little fish' while Mozart was playing.

So, although I've seen little weight loss with these, I've seen other benefits. Not having had Mark's spicy sausage in my mouth for more than a week being the first one to come to mind.

Five stars!

-Margaret

THE IDIOT GOVERNMENT REVIEWS

Read the first three reviews from the book:

Monsun 12V Hair Dryer

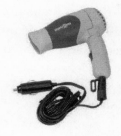

Much better than a towel.

Being an MP is an important job. We're beacons of the community. We're looked up to by many. This is why it's imperative to have good, strong hair. Fluffy, brushed and dandruff free. Although I will say: I don't condition it, I don't want it *too* fluffy. People would think I wanted to be a woman. I wash my hair almost daily. I allow myself a day off on Saturdays.

I keep this hairdryer in the car as I find by the time I've driven to the train station my hair is at the optimum dryness needed to obtain the desired, strong look. The dryer itself is a little diamond. Plugs right into the cigar lighter of my Jaguar and I'm able to store it in the glove compartment right in between my box of tissues and expenses book. The power output is everything needed to blow dry your bonce in a car park. People have walked past laughing before now, but why would I care what they think? I bet they all voted Labour anyway.

The dryer has its uses elsewhere, too. I spilt my coffee over myself as I was getting off the train late one night, and *yes* it was <u>definitely coffee</u>, not as the local rag reported, urine. I was sober and I stand by that fact, unequivocally. There is absolutely no truth in the story that I wet myself while asleep on the train. I wouldn't have been near my car if that was the case. Anyway, enough of that, I found myself with the need to dry my trousers and this little diamond presented itself for the task. After ten or fifteen minutes of thoroughly drying my wet crotch I realised that my underpants were also sodden, as was a little of the shirt that was tucked in. As it always is — I'm smart in my presentation, not like some of these liberal pansies who flounce about in corduroy and claim they're special because they've never had rubber soles in their flip flops.

Being a stickler in my quest to look good for the general public, I decided the only thing to do was whip off my trousers and dry my smalls — and I'm not including the little Dangly in that. * Massive Wink * The coffee was a large cup and had really soaked into the cotton, it took ages of waving the machine over the pants for them to dry. The heat that kicked out of this small machine was enough to heat up the liquid before it dried it. It got to the point where it was burning. I decided the best thing to do before putting on the golf trousers

I had in the boot was to remove my hot, wet pants and dry them properly. I needed pants, there is no way I could have gone commando, I'm not French. I'm also not stupid, I wasn't going to stand in the car park as naked as a new born, of course not. I climbed into the back of the Jag, removed my pants and started to dry myself liberally.

After a couple of minutes of feeling the refreshing heat in my nether regions, and just as I was really making sure that little Dangly was dry, the car filled up with what I first thought was a strobe light — like the kind you get at a roller disco. I couldn't believe it and I was right not to. It was a bloody photographer. The swine must have been stalking me or something. Being the coward he was, the Pap ran off.

Not one to be crossed I gave chase. Unfortunately, I forgot that I was naked from the waist down. I'd taken my shoes off in order to remove the wet trousers. I soon remembered I was barefoot when I ran over the gravel at the edge of the car park. As I was doing that strange dance you do when you walk on sharp stones in bare feet, the flashes started again.

A double whammy of bad luck then ensued: I realised I'd still got my hairdryer in my hand and that I'd snapped the lead. I also realised that the blue lights behind me didn't mean I'd wandered into a night club, but that the police had turned up. *No problem,* I thought, *I own these guys, I have dinner with their chief inspector every other Friday. They'll probably offer to arrest the photographer.* I couldn't have been further from the truth. They wouldn't listen to a word I said and attempted to arrest me.

Daniel Dangly doesn't go down without a fight in the House of Commons or anywhere else, and a train station car park is no different. Eventually, though, I was out of breath, and over powered. The officers wouldn't listen to my threats of having their jobs. I couldn't believe it. I'm not used to being treated like riff raff.

There were pictures being taken throughout. The paparazzi were there — cheering and calling out, never people to miss out on degrading someone better than them.

I grazed little Dangly on the gravel as I was hauled up. The poor little bugger was red raw. It hurt like hell. Not as much as the picture of me looking utterly ridiculous that appeared in the national papers the next day, though. The great Daniel Dangly standing there, crying, and only wearing the top half of a suit. That hurt more than any penis pain I may have been suffering from, or indeed any penis pain I think I could ever suffer. Even the kind that happens only in industrial accidents.

All charges: being drunk in charge of a vehicle, public indecency, and resisting arrest, were dropped, of course. My public image needed some serious work, though. It's a good job that once the editor of 'The Moon', Ms Rivers, had earned a decent amount out of the story, she was onside to help to discredit the photographer, the passengers on the train and the police, and make them all out to be the liars that they truly are. There may have been a tiny bit of truth in what some of them were saying, but not in the main, they were all jumping on the gravy train and taking things out of context, trying to get five minutes of fame by telling their 'story'.

Ms Rivers is good, though. She did an excellent job of hanging the photographer out to dry. He hasn't worked for any of the red tops since. I think there were some naughty pictures found on his work computer, too. If that's the type of person he was, it's no wonder he had no problem with stalking me, stealing my clothes and then photographing me in my moment of distress. My public image has been restored, regardless of what a couple of policemen say in statements — they've all been pulped anyway.

The officers concerned will be too busy pushing pens to upset any more of the Tory party with silly little vendettas against the leader of their local council.

It's a good Job the PM went to school with Rivers' lesbian lover or it might have been hard to get the press on side with this one.

The judge in the photographer's assault trial ordered him to pay damages for a new hairdryer. I bought the same model, as before it was rudely snatched from my hand and smashed it was a great little tool. The compensation is enough to keep me in new Jaguars for a few years to come.

I even use this model dryer to get myself dry after I've showered in my London office, too. It's better and much more luxurious and comfortable than using a towel. I was able to put it through expenses, along with the plug adapter for a wall socket.

- Daniel Dangly

The Best Prank Book Ever! [Paperback]

Great for getting the angry person in your office back!

Being a secretary for the Chief Whip in this government has very few perks. In fact, I struggle to think of more than one. The one I do have is that I get to make his life a little more difficult than it could be. It's my one pleasure in this job. My admin team are good as gold and do most of the work that is put to me. On the whole we give him very little to moan about. That doesn't stop him having one of his enormous tantrums most days, though. We've got a little bet going — on the amount of times he swears in one sentence. Seriously, these posh public school types swear more than any squaddie I've ever met. I've got my bet set on every other word, I've won a few times too. The team have shorter amounts of swear words for their bets, although no one has between one and three, there is just no chance he would stoop as low as that in a paddy.

He's drunk most days by 2 p.m. Some lunch or other with one of his old school pals usually descends into an afternoon of brandy and cigars in front of some fireplace or other — normally in someone's office or chamber. That's the best time to prank him.

We ran out of pranks after the absinthe in his coffee, plus some of the more junior workers, who hadn't been subjected to as many tizzy-poos as the rest of us, thought that making him sick up burning fluid from his nose was a bit too much.

That's when I suggested they think of some other stuff. This book was a birthday present to me from one of the girls. I have to say, having this in the office has certainly upped the amount of swearing. I could be in with a chance of winning the bet at this rate. One of the best was when we changed all his appointments round on the same day the IT bods were upgrading the server. He left in the morning thinking he had a clear afternoon and, as always, returned around four, drunk, to make sure there hadn't been too many important emails from the PM before getting changed into his cycling shorts and heading home. However, what he didn't realise was that the Home Secretary and the PM were coming for a meeting at 4.15. He was just pulling up his tight shorts when they walked in. I managed to see a little of his reaction as he realised what day it was before I closed the door, as I always do when leaving. He looked like a pathetic child who'd messed himself and been caught trying to change himself before he was old enough to. The PM and Home Secretary left the room shortly after I heard raised voices, looking a little flustered.

The next day I won the bet on swear words. I think one of the IT blokes got it worse than we did.

- Ann Hathaway

Personalised Pen and Case

A splendid symbol of power amongst the normal people in your office.

It's very important as an MP to look like you know what you're doing. You need to look the part at all times. I bought this for my first day in the big house. As Member of Parliament, it's important to have the correct stationery. I owe it to my constituents. I owe it to myself.

Getting it personalised was easy. I simply sent the seller my requirements, 'Elouise Munch, MP for South West Cambridgeshire' and it was delivered a few days later. I've kept the receipt ready to put in with my first expenses claim. Sadly, though, as it was from Amazon there is a digital record of it so there's no way I can doctor it with my new pen, which means the time I spent ordering it won't be covered.

Once I was in the office, the pen out and on display, I could see everyone that I came into contact with was impressed. I'll only really need the pen for ticking boxes, signing autographs and such like. I've got my own secretary and a PA for all the boring stuff. It's where I've always wanted to be, in charge. I've got all the gophers I need. Anything I want doing they have to do.

After the first day introductions were done, I headed over to 'The Big House' for the first cabinet meeting. Having a chat with Perry, the new Minister for Transport, was interesting. He filled me in on the job. Which is basically: turn up to the Chamber, jeer a bit, wave some paper round, then do a couple more meetings, order the team to do the work leading on from the meetings, then lunch with whoever takes my fancy that day and whack the whole lot on expenses. It's pretty much everything I've ever wanted. All the power, a bit of pocket money to fund my lunches as I work my way up to the House of Lords and pretty much anything paid for by the stupid tax payer through the expenses system.

It all starts with this pen.

- Elouise Munch

PETE SORTWELL

MORE VILLAGE IDIOT REVIEWS

Read the first three reviews from the book:

TCP Original Antiseptic Liquid 200ml

Just don't put on the sore patch that used to be your nipples.

I'll start by saying: I bought the Spanish version of this. But it was still called TCP, how amazing is that!? I did fear that they'd have called it something else and I'm so glad they hadn't.

I found myself in need of this while on my honeymoon. Which wasn't something I'd planned for, but then I don't suppose anyone ever planned the need for TCP, unless they were drastically weird or something — which I'm not.

Once all my employees had left I changed into my shorts and navy singlet, wolfed down the honey sandwich, strapped on my Hi-Tec silver running shoes and headed out into the summer night.

As is the norm in Spain, I hired a little moped. Mary, my new wife, refused to come with me on a trip to the local monastery. The moped I hired wasn't in the best condition but, as Pedro informed me, the leopard-skin seat made up for any mechanical shortcomings. He was right, too; everyone was looking at me as I chugged my way through the local town. Mind you, I think the young ladies might have been looking at me just as much as they were looking at the sex-mobile that I was riding.

Seeing as I was on holiday I wore the uniform all vicars wear when out of sight of their flock — Speedos. The smaller the better, we all wear them on holiday; well, after a long year of wearing our robes and tight-necked dog collars, a small pant-like trunk is extremely liberating. I could feel the wind on the inside of my thighs, airing Jesus and the two disciples, Peter and Nathanael. I bloody loved it. The only thing that would have made it better was my old large hip flask, but seeing as Mary had pronounced me an alcoholic, I wasn't allowed it on the holiday.

The monastery was at the top of a mountain so I was soon out on the open road. Getting up the hill took a little longer than if I'd been walking, but it was steep so I was happy that I didn't have to actually walk, and I managed to ignore the kids that strolled past me as I was crawling up the hill on Pedro's trusty moped. They were just jealous that I was burning my bare feet on metal and not on the road like they were.

Meeting the Spanish vicars was nice. I couldn't understand a word they were saying, but we pointed at the Bible and nodded in agreement a fair amount. After tea it was time to head back down the hill. Unfortunately, this was when I found the brakes weren't all they should have been and I got the speed wobbles. Luckily I was only on the first corner so wasn't going as fast as I imagine I would have been if I'd careered all the way down. I still hit the ground at some pace, though, and it seemed for a while that the pace would continue. That part of the road had recently been tarmacked, so was fairly smooth for me to skid on. I didn't feel the pain until I'd stopped and the heat from the road brought me out of the daze I was in. My Speedos had disintegrated somewhere along the way. I'd been on my front as I skidded and looking down, I noticed that the little Pope had lost some of his skin. It wasn't until later I realised that I'd lost most of my nipples, too. In the police car that took me home I caught a glimpse of my chest in the mirror. Next thing I know I'm waking up with the bed sheets my wife had lovingly placed over me stuck to me! The pain started all over again.

Mary had also forgotten to get holiday insurance, so with no choice but to take my healthcare into my own hands, I headed down to the chemist to see what I could lay my hands on for under five Euros. (I'd spent all my holiday money on the moped rental.)

I think the chemist must have been a sadist or something because the smile that appeared on his face when I showed him my scarred body was not something I expected. The smile grew as he handed me the bottle of TCP and waved his hand in dismissal when I offered him payment.

When you go on holiday, you don't expect to have to deal with the police once, let alone twice. I'd almost stopped screaming by the time they arrived at the villa. Apparently they were responding to reports of a little girl being murdered. In my defence, it wasn't like if you hurt yourself normally, this pain got worse as time went on, even if you weren't dabbing the area with a TCP-soaked bit of cotton wool.

Thankfully it was the second but last day of the holiday, so I didn't have long to wait before I could see a British doctor who didn't demand payment upfront before he let me take my T-shirt off. Unfortunately for me, scabs had started to form by then and he had to tear them off to get the bits of gravel out of my body that had lodged there during the accident. When I left the surgery I asked if there was anything I needed to do with the wounds while they healed. His answer? TCP. I didn't say anything, though, as us vicars aren't allowed to swear.

I kept the bottle of TCP and it's come in handy for the locals. Jock knocked our door late one night; something had bitten him, so I lent him a bit of this. I was glad to see that he screamed like a little girl, same as I did when I first applied it. Jock is an old biker chap so it means I'm not as soft as the people who were laughing at me thought I was.

-Father Frederick

Become a Scottish Laird/Lady

Born into money but no title? This is for you.

Monty's the name, lording is the game. Which, to be honest, is a little troublesome if you don't have the title of 'Lord'. I'm rich, sure. But due to an upsetting incident in 1951, in which my father accidentally hit Winston Churchill in the corkers with a croquet mallet, he wasn't given the title he'd been promised. It was all wrong and if Churchill hadn't been so much of a bloody hero, the papers would have been all over the fact he took a large amount of money from my father to fund his last political campaign. All this meant that there was no title to come to me with the house and land in my inheritance. My father never got over the fact that he was to die like a normal man; we told everyone we were Lords. In fact the Sheptons have been telling people that for centuries, and until that fateful game of croquet, we were in line to be actual Lords. Father said he'd even been promised his own sword, too, so it was a double loss for him. Me? I've got my gamekeeper, Chopper, so I don't need a sword. Any trouble, I just point him at it and let him off his lead. Metaphorical lead, that is. You're not allowed to keep your own staff tied up in this day and age.

As I said, I've got it all; heirlooms from the ages, most touched or owned by people of substance. My gamekeeper, Chopper, is always getting his hands on things to add to the collection. I've a feeling he's a very good cat burglar and when we get back from a shoot somewhere he'll always produce something that I know not to ask questions about. I pay him well for it and add to the family collection of antiques and relics. This title really was the only thing that was missing from my life.

So once this wondrous thing called the Internet came out, I finally ended the age-old family tradition of getting ripped off by people who claimed they could sell us a title. I found this little beauty and can you believe the price! Under fifty new pounds — to be a Lord!

I purchased it in no time. Apparently all you do is purchase a square centimetre of land in Scotland and under law you're allowed to call yourself a Lord. Brilliant. I got straight on the phone and bought a square mile. It means I've bought all the other centimetres that people have bought from this company and that they can't now call themselves Lords, but then it shouldn't be the case that anyone with fifty pounds can do it. You should have years of wealth in your bloodline, land, cattle, a gamekeeper. So not only I am Lord of my own manor in the village where I live (I won't name it as there are more than a hundred ex Lords and Ladies that would quite like to know where I live at the moment), I'm also a living Lord in Scotland. I'm considering sending Chopper up there and seeing if he can pull a band of men together to build me a castle. Although I think castles are quite expensive these days and I don't want to have to sell any of the artwork, so it might be a project for a couple of years' time.

Being rich, I also opted for the cufflinks with the family coat of arms. We've had our coat of arms since Nelson drew them on a scrap of paper (before he lost his drawing arm) in whatever year it was Nelson lived. Just another little bit of background to my story and how, if you are one of the people who have lost your title, you should really feel grateful that someone from such good stock as me now holds it.

So if you're reading this and you are one of those people, all I can say is I'm sorry. I don't mean it, but I'm sure you understand that I'm better than you and deserve it more. Let's face it, you were probably punching well above your weight by calling yourself a Lord in the first place.

I will tell you, though, it feels great to be an actual Lord rather than a fat old fraud.

Tally ho!

-Monty

Safari Aero Javelin 600g

You need to choose this OR a stick. Never both.

I recently bought the Safari Aero javelin, it's something that I've been meaning to take up since school. I used to like a bit of shot-put too, but I had to stop that after I accidently messed my pants during the village version of the Highland Games. They're just too heavy and at my age, you just can't trust a fart enough to be throwing heavy things around from a squatting position — especially not when you're wearing a traditional Scottish kilt, with no underwear. It still hurts me to talk about. Ethel, the local crazy, was seen stuffing the kilt into her bag after I'd discarded it into the nearest garden.

So as you can see, my need for lighter things to throw was somewhat urgent. I read the product description with great interest; however, I'd like to let people know that if, like me, you go on YouTube for tips and you see a video that advises you to use a stick to practice with before you take up a javelin, please listen to my experience of it. I watched the video. The wait for the Safari Aero was fairly long, so I popped over the road to kick down some of Brian's trees to use for sticks. (It's OK because no one likes him, so even if they saw me doing it, they wouldn't have told him.) Then I went out in the park behind the Co-op to practise. I think I got the stance down to a tee within the first ten throws on the first day, then I was out every day, as much as I could. I even felt my aim and strength improving. I'd sprayed a target onto the hedge and it caught the sticks; it was a fairly robust thicket.

You can imagine my enthusiasm for the actual javelin pole to arrive, and after the allotted three weeks, it did. I'd got a matching vest for the big day and slipped the singlet on in double-quick time and headed out to the park. This is where my gripe comes in: the javelin is actually a lot lighter and more aero-dynamic than a stick, so when I threw it, it went sailing over the hedge and beyond, into the Co-op car park. By the time I got round there, it had gone. No doubt Ethel had seen it and taken it home to train runner beans up. I'd go round and challenge her, but she's been known to carry a police baton, and to bite.

Personally I feel hurt by the whole situation and have decided to go back to throwing sticks, although I'll have to find a new garden to get them from as I've taken all the branches from Brian's trees.

So, my advice to you if you're thinking of buying one of these bad boys, is wait for it to come, don't bother with the sticks, or just throw sticks instead. Whatever you start with, stay with.

-Jock

PETE SORTWELL

DATING IN THE DARK: SOMETIMES LOVE JUST PRETENDS TO BE BLIND

Read an extract from the book:

Prologue

'You look like the scrambled version of Humpty Dumpty — *after the accident*,' — is probably the worst insult I've ever had thrown at me.

As it was my own mother who threw it, I think it hurt more. Since her dementia had developed, her blatant disregard for mine or anyone else's feelings had become more and more prominent. Mind you, thinking back, I hadn't even known she was ill when she'd shouted the insult up the stairs as I trudged to my room after yet another failed date. If I had known, I wouldn't have moved out and left her to the mercy of her carers, but back then she was still going to the shops on her own without being brought home by the police for using supermarket aisles as toilets.

I'm Jason Harding. I'm ugly. I know I'm ugly. I'm told I'm ugly and the results of seven hundred and thirty five unsuccessful dates have confirmed that I'm simply not attractive to the female of the species. It's all quite depressing, really.

CHAPTER 1

'You know what your problem is, don't you?' My best mate Barry said one day over a coffee.

'No. That's just it, I don't,' I told him, amazed that after years of consoling me he still thought I knew why it was that girls would rather change their phone number than speak to me again.

'You're looking in the wrong places,' Barry told me, raising his eyebrows in a knowing way before taking a sip of his drink.

That was it, there was no more wisdom in Barry than that. *You're looking in the wrong places.* No suggestions as to where I should look, no inside knowledge on the matter, just *you're looking in the wrong places.* With friends like that, it's no wonder I felt like chucking myself under a bus.

Barry had been in the same boat as me until a couple of years back when he struck lucky and managed to convince Mandy, the girl who took the coats at the bingo hall, that having him move into her place and eat all her food for the rest of her life was a good idea. Since then he's been convinced he knows everything there is to know about dating and women. He doesn't, though, he was as hopeless as me up until he met her, and it wasn't all plain sailing from the get-go with Mandy, either. He had to pretty much stalk her before she even noticed him. Barry never even liked bingo, but he was more than happy to drag me along to watch him completely ignore the game and just sit in our little booth staring at Mandy as she tried to busy herself and pretend she wasn't being stared at by the second ugliest bloke there that night. After a couple of months of Barry's eyeballing campaign, Mandy finally gave in and agreed to go out with him for a plate of Chinese food. As it turned out, Mandy was interested in the same weird little Japanese cartoons that Barry was. Instantly they had a common bond, something to talk about and something to share.

It's situations like that which make me think there is something in all this fate business. People who believe in fate think that everyone's life is already mapped out, that it's already there and just waiting to be lived. I mean, how can two fairly regular people, not the best lookers and into the same cartoons, find each other just like that? It was like a tractor beam, they weren't wearing special Manga T-shirts or badges or anything, something just brought them together. Fate. It must be fate. It got me thinking, also, that fate *must* have been against me; either that or my fate was to be alone, forever.

'Where should I be looking then, Barry?' I asked, after having worked myself up into one thinking about fate.

'In the right places, of course,' Barry said, making me feel like belting the hot chocolate I was nursing into his stupid big head. After another sip of his coffee he continued. 'Work out what you're into, things you like, then go to places where those things happen. It's not as if you have hobbies, is it? Get one and you're golden.'

This was a lie. I did have a hobby. All my time was spent on it, too. I didn't have many interests other than finding a girlfriend, and I don't suppose that'd be something a woman would fancy discussing. Unless she was a lesbian, and then I'd have been in the wrong place, I suspect.

'That's not a hobby, that's an obsession,' he told me when I reminded him how much time I had put into my 'hobby'. 'And one that's driving you crazy,' he added.

He was right, too. I was going crazy. I very much doubt there was anyone as unlucky in the love department as me, not that lived in the community, anyway. I mean, even guys on death row still managed to find someone to love; fair enough, it was through letters or a slight change of persuasion, but they still found someone.

There was nothing I could do but concede to what Barry had said. Other than drink my hot chocolate and try and think about things, other than women, that I liked.

'Come on, let's see what you've got,' he said, ferretting an old shopping receipt out of one pocket and a bookies pen out of the other. Together we hammered out a list of things that I'd shown interest in during my life so far:

1. Fish and chips

2. Feeding the ducks

3. WWF wrestling

4. Going to the dry ski slope and seeing people fall over

5. Duck Hunt on the NES

6. Writing my name on walls

7. He-Man

8. Skimming stones

9.   Watching people fall over on YouTube

10.   Women

I vetoed Barry's suggestion that I enjoyed collecting my school bag from gardens after he'd chucked it over on the way home from school. As you can see from the list, there wasn't much there that could be transferred to a joint interest with a woman, unless she was a computer game-playing bi-sexual interested in shooting, throwing and fatty food. Which, as desperate as I may have been, didn't sound very appealing.

'But what do you like *now*?' Barry kept asking in between adding items to the list. My answer was invariably, women. Although I have to admit my love of fish and chips hasn't waned since childhood. I eat it at least three times a week. Cod, chips and a nice big dollop of mushy peas. Bloody lovely it is. I'd dream that if I ever did get a girlfriend, I'd take her into the local chippy and show off how well known I am in my area. I just have to show my face and my food is wrapped and ready to go. Barry said this wasn't something that would impress a girl, but I'm not so sure, I've seen plenty of women in the shop getting the same meal, with or without mushy peas, AND I'd pay for hers ... that's got to be a plus point.

'Well, fish and chip obsessed women are few and far between, there must be something you like doing that involves meeting women. Even something you've always thought about doing but have never done?' Barry asked, after clicking his fingers a couple of times to wake me from my fish and chip day dream.

'I'd quite like to go on a booze cruise one day,' I told him. 'Come to think of it, we've always talked about going on one.'

'Christ, this isn't getting us anywhere, is it?' Barry said, getting stressed and holding onto his nose like it was about to fall off and only his thumb and forefinger could stop it happening. 'Look.' He laid his palms flat on the table. 'Do you think it's because you're ...'

I cut him off.

'It's not because I'm short. Women aren't only attracted to tall men. It's not like I'm a midget or anything, is it? So no, it isn't because I'm short,' I told him, digging my heels in on that particular argument.

It's true, I am short. I'm not *that* short, though. To be a midget, dwarf or any other derogatory term people like to use for people that aren't as tall as most people, you need to be under four foot ten and I'm four foot ten and a half, which is over one centimetre or ten millimetres more than that, so it's clear that I'm not a midget. Also, I knew that before the Internet was invented, so that proves I'm right and in fact, very knowledgeable on the subject. Too many people rely on the Internet for information these days. It's unreliable, Google is the worst place to look if you need to find something out. Don't even get me started on Wikipedia. I mean, what sort of knowledge source lets any old Internet psycho enter whatever they like as 'fact'? It's ridiculous. I have a set of encyclopaedias, bought them a few years back. They're much better and more factual than most of the shit on the Internet. It's actually quicker to get the book I need off the shelf, flick through the pages and find what I need than it is to look on the Internet for hours, find the answer, then check and double check that it's correct. My encyclopaedias are all I need. The computer I have is just used to find women.

'Why don't you try speed dating? There's got to be someone out there for you and I think that's the best way to go,' Barry said.

'Tried it, didn't work,' I said, thinking back to the disaster that it had been on the occasions that I had tried it.

'Yeah, but that's how you fail. Giving up gets you nowhere,' Barry explained hitting a chord within me. It's true, I do give up on things fairly easily. Not the entire goal, but the various different ways of getting to it. I have been known to stop trying if something doesn't work the first or second time. Take dating websites, for example; I've joined up and paid a year's fee on more than I care to remember, then after experiencing a couple of dire dates, just packed it in and looked for another one. I suppose I'm just too keen.

'Will you come with me?' I asked Barry.

'Absolutely not, my friend. I've got a bird. No need for places like that.'

'Nice,' I replied, not appreciating Barry's attempt at a joke. 'I'll try it again, but I want to go to a different one this time, Last time it was soul-destroying, I couldn't face seeing the woman who ran it again. I mean, surely it's rude to tell "the only person she's ever met to get no interest whatsoever" that he is just that?'

'I think it could be rude. But it's a little bit funny in a tragic kind of way though, you've got to admit that,' Barry said.

'It would be if it wasn't me she'd said it to,' I confirmed.

It had been tragic. Now, for those that don't know what speed dating is, I'll explain; the organisers get an equal amount of males and females in a room, then on the night one group is selected, usually the females, to go and sit at a table. Then the men have to go and sit at each of the tables in turn and 'sell' themselves to the woman. They get two minutes with each woman, then an alarm or bell sounds and the leader shouts 'Change' and the men all move clockwise to the next table and do the same thing again.

On that particular evening I'd sat down opposite a woman who was pretty average-looking. Someone who I would have expected to need speed dating to get a look-in. She was almost spilling over the chair she'd managed to perch on and her face wasn't so much disfigured as lopsided. I have to admit, I wasn't really impressed on first sight, but being the gentleman that I am I decided I'd give it my all and see if I could see past the folds in her face. I discovered that she worked in a bakery, that she still lived with her grandmother and that she didn't want to be doing either of those things, but as the council wouldn't give her a flat of her own and *Hello* magazine wasn't looking for writers that couldn't spell, she was going to be staying in the bakery for the duration (of her life probably). I, in turn, informed her that I was a car salesman — I'd decided to lie and that was the first thing I thought of. I could have been anything, but I chose that. My brain clearly decided to work against me that day. I decided not to tell her the real truth about my job. It would only either disappoint or disgust her, no one likes insurance companies or the people that work for them.

I told her proudly that I did have my own place, paid for by me, and I added, 'I'm allowed to have anyone I like over.' I raised my eyebrows up and down as I said it. It didn't have the desired effect, though, she just sneered. As did every other girl I tried to impress with that particular fact; one even called me a wanker before turning away in her chair and refusing to talk to me for the last one minute, forty seconds of our 'date'. The over-exaggerated sigh and shift in her chair alerted half the room to the fact that my date with Karen, number 7, wasn't going well, and I think this had an effect on the overall outcome of my night. After I'd sat at thirty-five tables for two minutes each and given my all trying to impress every single woman there (and hopefully persuade one to come back to my place) I waited in a quiet corner of the bar while the forms we'd all filled in were looked through for a match.

How it works is the leader of the group gets you to tick boxes on your way round the room, 'yes', 'maybe' or 'no interest', then her computer processes the information and comes up with two people that are matched either in the 'yes' or 'maybe' columns and the corresponding results are sent via email, along with the relevant people's contact details and a picture so you can remember who's who. When I was filling out my form, I decided to forget how Karen had ignored me and give her a chance anyway. I ticked 'maybe' for her and 'yes' for everyone else. Now, although you have to wait until you either get home or get your smart phone out (if you're a tosser) to see who was interested, you could see how many matches there were. My card? Zero matches. No maybes and no yesses. That was when the leader, Zoe, as high on life as she had been all evening, delivered the killing blow that she'd never had such a dismal failure of a man darken her speed dating door.

'Not everyone finds love here, but I've never had not one single show of interest in a person before. Even big Linda, she's one of the regulars, usually shows interest in all the men in the hope of finding love. You must have said something really awful,' Zoe told me.

'Oh,' I replied. There wasn't much else to say, although there wasn't that much time to think about it as Zoe had more encouraging remarks to make.

'I'll have to change my advert now,' she said putting her bottom lip out in a way that made me think she was fairly sexy.

'Or you could show interest,' I suggested hopefully.

'Oh. Oh, no, Jason. Sorry, but …' Zoe said, looking down at me, 'just, no,' she finished, before walking off, shaking her head.

As I left, I saw her necking a shot and I'm fairly sure it was the thought of me that made her shudder rather than whatever it was in the glass.

Once I'd finished reminding Barry of how much of a complete waste of time speed dating was, not to mention the little bit of my soul that I'd left in the back room of the Pig and Whistle that night, he had a suggestion.

'Find one with an angle. There must be different types of dating places, we've already established that speed dating gets the highest ratio of people seen in the lowest amount of time, so find a speed dating evening that has an angle.'

'What, like speed dating for munters?' I asked.

'Well, you said it. Basically, yes.'

'But I don't want an ugly girl, given the choice. I want a pretty one who'll accept me for who I am and maybe, just maybe, sleep with me just once. Or more than once,' I told Barry, laying out the terms I'd just invented for this plan. 'More than once would be better.'

'Well, therein lies the problem,' Barry said, draining the last of his coffee. 'You want a pretty girl, but even the ugly, fat ones that still live at home don't want anything to do with you. This is what I meant by an angle.'

'Yes, but you've not told me what angle, Barry! You're just sitting there talking about how I should do things just because you finally managed to get out of the hole that I'm in. Doesn't mean that I'll be able to find someone, no matter how much you talk about angles!' I shouted.

'Ooooooh. Mr Touchy. It's not my fault you're in this situation, is it?' Barry retorted, also getting pissed off.

'Oh, don't give it all that. You're always playing the "*it's not my fault*" card.'

'Well, this isn't. You're the one who can't find a girl, I'm just trying to help. It's clear you're not interested in listening, this is why you're struggling. Your way doesn't work and you're not prepared to listen to anyone else.'

'You haven't fucking suggested anything!'

'I have. I said you should ...' Barry started, but I cut him off.

'Fuck off, Barry.'

'Say what?'

'You heard, just fuck off, I've had enough of you,' I told him, seething. Seething not so much at him, but at the situation. I should've never discussed it, I knew it would piss me off.

'I'll tell you what I'll do: I will fuck off, and you can shove it, you miserable old git,' Barry said, getting up and putting on his coat. 'And I'll tell you something else for free, you need a deaf, dumb and blind woman, that's the only sort I can see putting up with you, you ugly, short-arsed whinger.' And with that Barry strode out of the coffee shop leaving me to snap a couple of wooden coffee stirrers in an attempt to make myself feel better — it didn't work.

Barry could stay in a strop, he was like that sometimes. He'd calm down once he'd had no human contact other than with his bird for a week. He did have a point, though. A blind girl. She wouldn't be able to see I was ugly, or short. It was the perfect solution.

Well, they do say *lose a friend, gain a new plan*. What's that? They don't? Well, they will now. I might write in to the publishers of my encyclopaedia and suggest they add it to the inspirational quotes.

BRIDE AND GLOOM: SOMETIMES LOVE IS BETTER OFF BLIND

Read an extract from the book:

Prologue

Pretending to be blind to get a woman was equally the stupidest and bravest thing I've ever done. Stupid, in that I thought I'd fool anyone into believing I was, but brave, just for the fact of trying and the sheer audacity of my ploy. Plus, on top of that I met Emma, my beautiful fiancée, so in the grand scheme of things, I'm actually pretty clever, if you think about it.

Since I came clean and took the dark glasses off, things have been good, not GREAT. I wouldn't want to be the one to liken it to a superhero being unmasked – I'll leave that to others – but it's been refreshing and the new life I have now is something much better than I've had before. Ever.

Like with most relationships, we've come a long way and have committed to spending the rest of our lives together. This is the story of the lead up to the big day.

Chapter 1

'You've got to have a stripper, though,' my best friend Barry said, shoving another handful of chips in his gob.

'I don't think I *have* to, though, do I? I mean, what if Emma finds out?' I asked, making him pause before he was able to shovel yet another mouthful of Terry's finest in.

'Don't you think she'll be having some big muscly guy taking his kit off in front of her and waving his schlong in her face on her hen night, then?' he said, dangling his jumbo sausage in front of his own face as a prop, before taking a bite of it then shuddering when he realised what he'd made himself look like.

'It'd be a bit pointless, mate. She wouldn't see it, would she? She's blind, remember?' I told him.

'How could I forget? I helped you fool her into thinking you were, too,' he told me.

'So did I,' Terry shouted out from over the counter. I knew it was a bad idea to eat our food 'in'. Terry's always getting involved in other people's business, he's never changed.

Barry and I moved our heads closer together and carried on the conversation.

'Do you think it'll be a more touchy feely affair, then?' Barry asked, dropping his sausage and grabbing the air in front of him with both hands.

'Oh, that's funny, isn't it. I suppose you'll be going on stage next, making the masses laugh? Anyway, you were miming breast-groping then; she's not having any stripper, and even if she did, it wouldn't be a female one.'

'Oh, I know that,' he confirmed, picking up his sausage again.

'You know what, Barry ...'

'Oh, will you stop your moaning, it was a joke. All I'm trying to say is that it's 2014. Everyone has strippers for their stag or hen nights, it's the done thing. No one cares these days,' Barry reasoned.

'I don't think Emma would like me having one, that's what I'm saying. Plus, I wouldn't want to think about her being given a touchy feely dance by some six foot rugby player in the nude.'

'Gotta be better than having one off you, I reckon she'd thank her lucky stars she's blind if you started breaking out your moves. I remember how you used to move on the dance floor. It was like a cross between jogging on the spot and someone having some kind of arthritic flare up.'

'I'll have you know, I looked good,' I said. 'And anyway, you were no better, I remember you getting dragged out that club in Coventry after trying to impress the locals with your caterpillar.'

'They *were* impressed, it was them fascist bouncers that didn't like it. I was showing them up for the robots they were, that's why they dragged me out before I could even get up and apologise for kicking that woman in the face. I was too passionate, that was my problem.'

'You were too pissed, that was your problem.'

'What were we talking about?' Barry said, having found himself back in the room after a mental trip to Coventry.

'My stag night – you're supposed to be organising it,' I reminded him.

'Oh, yeah, I have. We'll be going paintballing with Terry, then fish and chips, then off out into town for a good old fashioned knees up, with a stripper thrown in somewhere along the way for a treat.'

'I keep telling you, I don't want a stripper,' I reminded Barry.

'Oh. OK, we *won't* have a stripper,' Barry said, doing one of his over-acted winks.

'No, seriously, I *don't* want one!'

'OK, *no stripper*,' he said, doing another wink. It was pointless trying to talk to him. I decided that I'd send him a text later, from home, explaining that it wasn't fair on Emma for me to be enjoying a stripper when she couldn't and that I wouldn't be paying for it out of the stag fund that I'd agreed to let Barry control.

I still don't think I was out of line in vetoing the stripper. It had only been a year since I'd come clean to Emma and told her I'd been lying and pretending I was blind. Sure, we knew each other pretty well these days, but in the face of everything I'd been through in order to find someone that was willing to marry me, I didn't think it was worth taking even the slightest chance of messing things up.

Before we left Terry alone to harass his normal customers for the evening, we needed to forget the banter and get on with the planning. Barry shared the list of people he'd thought of inviting along.

'So, we've got: me, you, Terry, Boris and Jerry. That's about it on the list of your friends. Shall I add my own friends or are you happy with the low numbers?' he said.

I laughed this off, but regardless of however brutal Barry was being, he had a point. Did I want that few on my stag night or did I want something altogether more extravagant? After all, I had my mother's money and it wouldn't be a problem if I did choose to have a bigger affair.

I thought about it and decided that I was more than happy to only have close friends there. I didn't need to fill my life with any more of Barry's weird manga cartoon friends. They were just too weird.

'So, just the small party, then. That's OK, more stripper for all of us,' Barry concluded, then had a thought. 'Hang on, what about Jerry? He's not going to be interested in a female stripper, is he? I'm not ordering a bloke in just for him, I refuse,' he told me, throwing his pen on the table and crossing his arms like he thought I might force him to actually hire a male stripper on my own stag night, just to keep the one gay bloke there happy. Although I did keep the idea in mind for later, should I feel the need to really upset him.

'I should think seeing as we're not having any kind of stripper it won't matter anyway,' I told Barry, reminding him what I'd been telling him for the last few weeks.

'Can I have Jerry's number?' Barry asked immediately. I knew his plan, he was the only one thick enough to think that I didn't.

'What for?'

'I need to check his size for the T-shirts, we're all going to be wearing them. Here, look, this is the picture I've had made for the back,' he said, getting out his iPhone and thrusting it in front of me.

'Jesus Christ, where did you get that? It's horrendous.'

'It's from when we went on that holiday to Greece in 1999, remember?' Barry said, looking at the picture like I should.

'I remember the holiday, I don't remember that picture, but why would I? I was passed out. I remember scrubbing off the beard you'd drawn on me, though.'

'Just be pleased I didn't remove your eyebrows,' he said, giving me a nod.

I remembered the holiday well. I still can't stand the feel of wire wool on my skin. It was our first lads' holiday, although I think 'lads' normally means more than two; nevertheless, two of us there were and we did have a good time. Barry still claims he had some other friends with him when he drew the beard on me. He didn't see them afterwards on any of the other nights out we had, though, and his story was patchy to say the least. He'd probably just got bored, as that particular night was the night of my nineteenth birthday and all the bars and pubs that we went to insisted on giving me free shots, and no matter how much they were watered down, the sheer number of them and the willingness of the reps to force them down my throat was too much for me. The last thing I remember is being involved in a 'drink a yard of ale' competition, standing behind the bar, wearing an apron with a fake pair of tits on it. I did manage to get it down me, but it all came straight up again. I'd have won if it hadn't been for the projectile vomiting.

'I am pleased, but I'm not sure they'd make this photo any worse than it is. You could have taken it when I had some clothes on,' I said, bringing myself back to the here and now.

'I could have put this one on there,' Barry said, pulling out a photocopy of an old Polaroid of me when I was four, standing up in the bath and weeing onto the floor. I remembered it well, it was taken by my father before he left us to it. Barry must have been going through my things at Mother's when we were cleaning up.

'I'm not sure I can pick out the worst of the two, they're both pretty bad. Do we really need T-shirts?' I asked.

'Of course, how else will people know you're the groom? Well, apart from the hat, but that just complements the T-shirt. They're going to be proper Fruit of the Loom shirts, nice ones, so don't worry,' he assured me.

'I know, I'm paying for them,' I reminded Barry.

'Well, your mum is.'

This was a point of Barry's, he liked to call my inheritance 'Mum's money'. Since she'd died and he'd helped get the carer that'd pushed her down the stairs sued, along with the company who employed someone with no qualifications, Barry had been much more content with himself. He used to see my mother as his own mother, or at least the closest to it that he'd ever had.

We were both in the position of being thirty with enough

money to live on for the rest of our lives. Barry's came from Social Services, through an abuse case that we weren't allowed to talk about, and mine came from inheritance, with more on the way from the care company. I don't think Barry meant any harm by calling it 'Mum's money', it was just his way of placing where he would be getting the money from. I've never been good with money, so with the old house sold and the rest of the estate in cash, I'd opted for a trust fund which Barry controlled and out of which he gave me enough to live on.

When the time was right, I'd move out of my house and in with Emma. We'd decided that I'd only move in permanently once we were married, although it didn't stop us staying with each other a lot of the time.

Terry came over and started cleaning away the plastic trays. He was excited that he was getting to take us paintballing. He even had a little pistol paintball gun underneath his white apron. I'm not sure how safe it was for a chip shop proprietor to be carrying live paint rounds when dealing with food, but once he'd passed the tray over the counter to the assistant he was employing that week (they all seem to bore quickly of his stories and leave within a week or two) he pulled it out and showed us. It was a funny shape, thin at the trigger end and getting wider at the end the balls came out of.

'It looks like a cock,' Barry observed, turning Terry's smile upside down.

'It's not a cock, it's a gun,' Terry confirmed, looking to regain his self-respect in the eyes of Barry. It was a non-starter, I don't know why he even continued the conversation.

'I know. But it looks like one,' Barry said, not giving up.

'You should be nicer to me, I'm the one sorting this all out; if it wasn't for me you'd still be staring at the noticeboard looking for something for us all to do,' Terry said, stopping short of putting his bottom lip out.

'There's only two things on your noticeboard. One is paintballing and the other is the failed campaign you tried to start last year to stop the bus stop being planted right outside your shop, and it's still only got your signature on,' Barry argued back.

Terry and Barry can argue. This is what it's like when you bring your friends together. If I've learnt one thing over the last year, it's that just because you like someone, it doesn't mean your friends will feel the same way. It's funny, me and Barry have known each other for most of our lives and I've known Terry for as long as I've been old enough to carry enough cash to buy a portion of cod and chips. I'd never really liked Terry that much before, I'd always found him to be a bit of a pain in the arse, but when he gave my other friend, Boris, a job after he lost his job as a taxi driver, I saw that he wasn't too bad after all. Barry wasn't of the same thinking, though. Terry was the local sad act in Barry's eyes and there wasn't much that would convince him otherwise.

Terry and Boris also bickered, although in theory they should have got on perfectly. Unfortunately Boris had a different opinion on health and safety to the rest of the world and thought nothing of drinking vodka while in control of all amounts of hot things. To be fair to Terry, he couldn't keep him on past the incident of a can of coke being thrown in the deep fat fryer 'to see if it popped'. That was the line that Boris crossed. Terry said he'd actually found the pickled eggs and pies that Boris had dipped in batter and chucked in fairly funny, but the coke exploded and covered the shop in some weird sticky oil/coke mixture. It was a good job it was before they opened one lunchtime or customers could have been treated to a face full of the delights of Boris's cooking. Boris was an idiot, he'd lost himself a lifetime of free food for the sake of a silly little experiment. Still ,he was still a regular in the shop and Terry didn't mind, as Boris had the uncanny ability to be able to listen to Terry's stories without getting bored. I suspect he is able to zone out easier than most.

However, I digress. I'd got two or three close friends and the dynamics of the group wasn't good. In fact, I was dreading spending the weekend with them.

'So, I sorted out the paintballing and you should be grateful. If it wasn't for me you'd all be going on one of those kids' days that the guys dressed in camouflage sell in the shopping centre. Just the fact they're wearing army fatigues in a mainly white building should tell you all you need to know about their knowledge on the subject. The one we're going on is excellent. I've tested it for you,' Terry told us, diverting the conversation away from his substandard noticeboard.

'I'm still not sure a day is enough,' Barry said, disregarding Terry's comment completely. 'I think we should go for a proper weekend, like every other normal male in the country does. I really can't see what your problem is with a weekend. It'll be great. At least we'd have time to relax and have a couple of drinks in between activities.'

'Just because,' I told him, not wanting to be drawn any further into the argument. I'd made my mind up and that was that, I didn't want to be on a God-awful weekend away with people that didn't like each other.

'Just because, you're a bender.'

'Oh, very mature. Very mature indeed. Well done, you've convinced me now. Calling me childish names has decided it. We'll go for the weekend.'

'Nice one, I'll book it up then,' Barry said, standing up. 'Terry, slight change of plan. I'll be in during the week to let you know if we're still going to your field for the paintballing or if it's at another one. And you'll need cover for the shop,' he shouted, as he almost ran out of the chippy. He was just being an arse, though, as he raised his voice higher than mine so Terry couldn't hear me complaining.

It wasn't until the next day when I got a text from him saying he'd booked us a minibus for the same weekend as Emma's hen do that I realised that he'd actually been enough of a dick to actually go and book somewhere. He, of course, used the stag fund. If there's one thing he knew for sure it's that I wouldn't want to lose the deposit money for four people.

I decided the only thing that it was in my power to do was give him the silent treatment, so I did that for a couple of hours before breaking and texting back to ask him where it was he'd booked it for.

'It's a surprise, trust your best man, he has your BEST interests at heart' was the only response I could get out of him. I warned him that Emma wouldn't be happy with him, but he called my bluff and lay down the ace card by informing me that he'd already run it by Emma via Jerry.

It was my night off from seeing Emma that night, so Boris came round after work. As I say, Boris had recently lost his job as a taxi driver, before losing it as a chip fryer. He's pretty much an alcoholic, but as he sees it, he's Russian and allowed to be. Lately he'd been working in a kitchen, just doing some washing up and trying to keep out the way of his wife as much as possible. Since the time he stole the family dog to lend to me, during 'the period of dishonesty' as Emma and I have come to call it, things had been pretty terrible for Boris at home. His wife, Yurtka, was stronger than any man I've ever had the pleasure of being punched in the face by, and nasty with it. I knew why Boris flinched whenever you walked past him or reached up to move your hair from your eyes, he was a nervous wreck. Said he couldn't leave her, though, due to having children with her. I suspect it was more about being scared she'd give him one more final beating if she ever caught up with him again.

'A weekend away sounds perfect to Boris,' he slurred. Oh, yeah, Boris had started talking about himself in the third person.

'I know it does to you, but you'll be luckily if you remember more than a few hours of the whole weekend. I'll have it imprinted on my brain, unable to cleanse it away, for years to come.'

'It sound to Boris that you don't want to go,' he told me, underlining my point about his short memory.

'I've been telling you for weeks that I didn't want to go for a weekend, we even agreed you could tell Yurtka that you were away for the weekend so you could stay here, instead. Can't you remember any of those conversations?'

'About what?' he asked, swigging the final dregs of wine from the bottle he'd brought with him. It was no good talking to Boris while he was this drunk. He just needed to get home and get some sleep. The new kitchen job was good for him, but I suspected they didn't stocktake the cooking wine very often. I let him nod off in the chair. He's never asleep long and it's amazing what a little bit of sleep does for a bumbling idiot — he's almost coherent when he wakes up.

When he woke up asking for a pint, I decided that I wouldn't mind one either. Having learnt the hard way, I knew better than to take Boris to the pub, so I just gave him twenty quid and told him to get a few cans from the shop. He returned twenty minutes later with a half bottle of vodka, four cans of Special Brew and a couple of cans of Stella, which he handed to me. Sometimes I still wonder what I was thinking giving him the money … mind you, what else did I expect? At least he'd got me something I actually liked.

We talked over Barry's plans for the stag night. It seemed I was the only one that didn't want a whole weekend away, or a stripper. Boris was extremely clear on his position on the stripper. He made sure that I understood he most definitely wanted one and, if possible, a nice Russian one with 'knockers her president would be proud of'.

I knew I needed to talk to Emma about the whole thing. I'd always had a tendency to keep things to myself (the fact I could see during the early stages of out relationship being a biggie). I just bottle it up and it's never good for me. Talking about stuff just wasn't something I was very good at.

That particular evening ended with Boris staggering about in the car park for an hour after he left my house and before he gave up and decided that he probably lived in the house that he had just come out of, and knocked back on the door. Before he passed out properly for the night, he underlined his need to have a weekend away from his wife and to see a stripper. Although his last words were:

'Boris needs sleep, hmm, boobs.'

THE DIARY OF AN EXPECTANT FATHER

Read an extract from the book:

Introduction

I thought I'd keep a diary; I'm never, EVER going to show it to anyone, but I am going to bury it in the garden, sealed in a tightly wrapped plastic bag. I'm even going to put a photo in. Then one day, in three thousand years' time, it'll be read by the aliens that take over the world and they'll have an insight into what life was like for someone who was becoming a father for the first time. They'll probably make me an alien lord or something. If DNA technology is advanced enough, they could even bring me back to life. If you are an alien warlord or anything like that, there is a sample of my blood on the piece of cloth sellotaped to the back of this diary. Please only recreate me if you plan on giving me an easy life. I've also put a strand of my best friend Keith's hair in the back; if you need to anally probe anyone then please use this to bring him back instead. I've always suspected he'd be really into that, so you'd probably be doing him a favour.

Other than that I'm Graham Peterson, I'm twenty-eight, and

it's the year 2012. If you're interested, England, where I live, is hosting the Olympic Games this year. That's a sporting event; or, more accurately, a series of sporting events. We're all completely underwhelmed. Most of London, our capital city, is closed off to make way for the people taking part, so normal people have to sit in traffic for far longer than they normally would.

Earth is a strange place at this time. You have to work all day for five days a week; we do this for most our lives and then we give up a couple of years before we die. I suppose you've moved on by now. Again, if you're able to recreate me into a world without work, then please do. I've a certificate in saving lives, so if any of your kind are planning on falling into swimming pools while wearing their pyjamas, I'm your man. For any other medical problems you're probably better off recreating someone else. David Attenborough might be a good bet.

Back to me, though … I'm an expectant father, I've not really got a clue what I'm doing and I thought writing this might give all your people in the future either an idea of how rubbish we were in the new millennium or go some way to helping me find a way out of my own worries. Either way it's a release for me and that's all I really care about.

So that's me. I'm a pretty normal guy who has found himself in a pretty normal situation. This is the story of the pregnancy and how I came to terms with being an expectant father.

Wednesday January 26th 2012

5.30 p.m.

I'm not quite sure what to do with myself. I remember seeing a TV programme about how writing a diary is a release and can help people. That's all I can think to do as I don't think this is something that can be sorted by my normal solution to problems (a few pints in the pub with Keith); this is going to be long term.

Alison rang me this morning and said she needed to speak to me urgently. I reminded her we were on the phone and that it was a technical possibility to speak there and then, but she insisted that we do it in person. I hate it when people do that, more so as I still had six hours of work left and couldn't help but obsess about just what it could be. I'm meeting her in an hour, so going to shower and get ready.

10.00 p.m.

Well, it's happened ... somehow I've managed to pass on my miserable seed to a woman who's kept it rather than rejected it, along with me, which is usually the case. Alison told me that she'd missed her period. I almost dropped my battered sausage. Why she waited until I was taking a bite to tell me, I don't know. I wasn't interested in carrying on eating after that, anyway. The shock was enough to put any man off a portion of Terry's excellent chips.

'How long have you known?' I asked.

'Well, I knew I'd missed it last week,' she told me.

After a few back and forth questions from me, which all

seemingly had really obvious answers, we decided that we had to know for sure and that meant one thing: pregnancy test. We spent an hour in Boots looking at all the different types. You wouldn't believe how many different sorts of tests there are, digital, non-digital, double digital, it's crazy. Pink ones, blue ones, white ones, I don't know how anyone is supposed to make the choice based on anything other than price. All of them were ninety-nine point something per cent accurate. I mean if it's five quid and ninety-nine point nothing per cent accurate, it's going to be pretty good, what real difference does the point four or point five make? There can't be much difference in it. I noticed the most expensive one was almost twenty-five quid. Just as I was jamming it back on the shelf before Alison saw it and wanted it, because of the shiny box and wild claims of being ninety-nine point NINE per cent accurate, a couple of greasy looking women walked past me and snorted, telling one another that, 'You can get the same thing in Poundland, only for a quid.' All smug. I don't believe you can actually get pregnancy tests in Poundland so I didn't drag Alison over there, but we did manage to settle on a middle of the road test for eight pounds. It's ninety-nine point four per cent accurate.

'Sir, you can't go in there,' the security guard called after me as I followed Alison into the ladies. I didn't think it would matter if it was for official business, no funny stuff or looking at women weeing. He wouldn't have it, though, and followed me in to remove me physically.

Alison didn't want to do it without me there, although personally I didn't mind too much. I wasn't really too keen on seeing her do *that* anyway. But if I've learnt one thing tonight then it's that you don't disagree with a pregnant — or at that point a potentially pregnant — woman. She'd been drinking water all the way into town and by the time we managed to get rid of the security guard from the shopping centre, Alison was really angry and literally busting for a wee. She frantically looked around the centre for somewhere to go. I couldn't see any other outcome than her wetting herself and was working myself up thinking about how today wasn't going at all as I'd thought it would when I woke up this morning. 'In here,' Alison demanded, almost pulling my arm out the socket as she clambered into a photo booth.

I couldn't fit into the booth, so I had to stand with my head poking through the curtain while Alison hiked up her skirt, pulled her pants. down and let the river flow, as it were. I was so busy concentrating on the stick to see if it lit up or beeped or whatever it was we were going to get for our eight quid that I didn't notice the river of urine that was pouring out the booth onto the floor, via my shoes. As quick as she'd started Alison finished and did the most inconsiderate thing I've ever known her to do: she flicked the piss stick and sprayed the only part of my body that was in the photo booth – my face. I got pregnant piss in my eyes, mouth and nose. I'd been given a golden face shower. I'm sure there are some weirdos out there that would have paid money to have a similar thing happen to them. I am not one of them.

It was as I stepped backwards that I noticed the river, well, I say noticed ... I mean slipped in. I had piss on my face and piss on my shoes. Then Alison said that we needed to wait five minutes for the test to dry. 'It'll probably be done in two,' I said wiping most of what had been on the stick off my face as we headed away from the mess we'd made as quickly as we could.

It wasn't a big celebration when the line stayed blue and the instructions told us that she was pregnant. If I'm honest, Diary, for one of the most important moments of my adult life, I was angry about having been covered in piss. So angry that all I could really think of was not that there would be a little bundle of joy in my life soon, but that I would be able to get home and have a regular shower designed for normal people soon. Alison just looked shocked. Then I don't suppose a girl grows into a woman thinking that she'll find out she's to be a mother after defacing a Kodak photo booth.

I walked Alison to the taxi rank, promised I'd call her tomorrow and came home to empty a bottle of Radox into my eyes.

I'm not sure how I feel really. Other than dirty, that is. I'll reassess in the morning.

1.00 a.m.

I've just woken up in a cold sweat. This is massive. How will I cope? What will I do? Can I afford it? How am I going to tell my parents? Life is going to change drastically in nine months.

Too many questions.

Thursday January 27th 2012

I hardly slept a wink after I'd woken up in a sweat. All I could think about was how there are so many ways in which I can screw this up. Alison seems so in control and with it. Well, she didn't sound scared on the phone, anyway, far from it. She sounded excited. We've only been together a few weeks. I hope I've not been trapped in a honey trap or whatever they call it these days. I've read about women like that in the paper. They get men into bed, get pregnant, and then latch onto them for life, like an evil stick insect.

I like Alison, I like her a lot. I mean I have to, she's the only woman who hasn't dumped me after three or four dates. Except for the incident with the piss yesterday, but I've decided to chalk that one down to experience and never again go anywhere near a photo booth while a woman, mine or anyone else's, is taking a pregnancy test in there. It's my own fault; I should have seen the danger in that situation. I was like a child wandering out into the road, no sense of the impending doom that awaited me. She's not a bad person, either. Anyone who looks after old people for a living can't be a bad person, She's also a qualified nurse, it's always good to have a nurse about the place.

Today dragged, I couldn't concentrate on the job in hand. Jane, my boss, started me off on the grill, which meant I had to cook all the bacon and have it ready for when the workers came in between seven and nine, then keep it going but also make sure that there was a supply of cheese on toast, too. It takes skill and timing to get it right when one is feeling OK with the world, and today I wasn't, which meant some of the workers got bacon that had only been cooked on one side, and the queue for cheese on toast was huge.

If the workers lean over the counter a bit they can see who's working the grill and tend to shout over 'Hurry the fuck up' if the cheese on toast isn't coming quick enough. I've told Jane that we need more grills in order to get the most popular item cooked and served quicker, but she's not made it happen. It's tense work and today I just couldn't do it. Once I'd dropped a tray of the stuff in front of the eyes of the very people waiting for it, Jane realised that if she wanted to get through the day without having to deal with endless complaints forms (which dictate our weekly bonus) it was time to move me to something less important.

That job was loading and unloading the dishwasher, which is the worst job in the kitchen and normally considered punishment. On the plus side, Boris was delighted to come off dishwasher duty and stop being punished for drinking the cooking wine three weeks ago. I think three weeks' washing up isn't punishment enough for drinking at work, but apparently dropping cheese on toast is worse than that. Still, I didn't have to deal with people shouting, or any scalding hot cheese that not only burns when it comes into contact with skin, but also sticks to it.

It's fair to say that today wasn't good. I spent the remainder of the shift loading and unloading the dishwasher. It was nice to have such a simplistic job, actually, as it allowed my mind to wander, but not too much. I went through the fears I had one by one and tried to think about them in a logical way. Here is my list of fears:

1. That I'll be a terrible father.

2. That the baby won't like me.

3. That I'll somehow screw up the kid so it ends up being a mass murderer or something.

4. That if the above happens, *The Sun* will do an investigation into the killer's family and expose me as a loser.

5. That Alison will run off with the baby and I'll be one of those fathers that doesn't get to see his kid until he dresses up like Batman and climbs something tall.

6. That I won't be able to afford a baby.

7. That it'll grow up and be like me.

8. That the baby will have a disability and be reliant on me for life.

9. That the baby will have ADHD and be an absolute nightmare.

10. That my nights will become even more sleepless.

When I've listed it like, that I'm glad I only went through them one at a time as that is a terrifying list to see all in one go.

Here is my rationale:

1. You might be, but everyone learns and there are classes on being a good father and loads of books you can read, doing this might just upgrade you from 'terrible' to 'mildly pathetic'.

2. Babies don't dislike people, they don't know how to. I can manipulate it into liking me.

3. See point 1, but also research on the Internet 'how to make sure your child isn't a killer'.

4. See points 1 and 3.

5. I'll have to ask Alison to marry me, she'll always be traceable then as she'll have my name.

6. I've thought more and more about this and if I marry Alison, then we'll live together and we'll have more money. Failing that, we could both give up work; I read all the time in the paper that people who don't work have more money than people who do. Failing that, I could stop spending all my money on myself. So there are options.

7. Of course it might. OR it might grow up and be like Alison. If we raise it like Alison then everything will be alright. Either that or I completely change my life around. I think it would be easier to raise it like Alison.

8. This is a natural fear all parents have, and most babies don't have disabilities or the human race wouldn't survive.

9. That'll be payback for me being a nightmare.

10. Ear plugs are cheap and Alison will be off work anyway, so she'll be happy to get up and look after the little one.

11. Just an extra: this is all months away. I don't need to worry so much. Nine months takes ages to pass.

Not a complete saviour of a list, but it certainly got me through the day at the dishwasher.

Alison has been on the phone this evening asking when we are going to make the news public. By 'public' she means telling her mum and then putting it on Facebook. I suggested we wait at least until we've been to the doctor's before we spoke to her parents, Alison wasn't so sure. Well, I say wasn't sure, she'd already told her mum, who in turn has told her dad. I think she did it last night as soon as she got home. I've not even met either of her parents yet. I suppose I'll have to at some point now.

I think I'll start another 'fears' list.

PETE SORTWELL

THE DIARY OF A HAPLESS FATHER

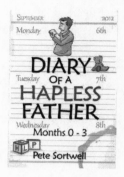

Read an extract from the book:

Introduction

This is my second diary. I've misplaced the first. I think Keith, my so called best friend, has stolen it. He's always struck me as a literature thief.

Just in case I don't find it again: I started the last diary as I was about to become a father. The mother of my baby, Alison, and I had only been together for a matter of weeks before she fell pregnant. It wasn't a recipe for success, but it seems to have worked thus far.

Tuesday September 25th 2012

5.00 a.m.

I've just got home from the hospital. Charlie Peterson is now with us. He's great. Tiny little ears, tiny little hands and big brown eyes looking up at the world. I read in my book that I bought to help me cope with the pregnancy that he can't actually see anything at the moment, but I'm not so sure, his eyes seem pretty focused to me. A little glazed, if anything, like a doughnut. He's got a full head of hair, too, more than me, even. I was holding him less than an hour ago. Alison and Charlie have headed down to the mother and baby ward now. I was told to go home and get some sleep as I'd started staggering about an hour after he was born. Mother and baby are OK, though, that's the main thing. The birth was awful, but I can't bring myself to talk about that now.

9.30 a.m.

So, the birth:

We arrived at the hospital about ten to nine yesterday morning. I'd not slept more than five minutes at a stretch as I was worried about what was happening next to me, although Alison seemed to sleep with no problems at all, only waking up once to move about a bit and go to the lav. In films the contractions seem to be a lot more violent than they were in reality; I still wasn't sure she was having them. But we were at the hospital, so everything was going to be OK.

Or so I thought. Once the obligatory three hours' wait had passed, the midwife on duty took one look at Alison (down there) and told us we needed to go home again until she was seven centimetres dilated. I was already pissed off before we even heard that, but the stony faced cow's standard 'don't care, I've said all I'm saying' response to every attempt I made to get her to change her mind really wound me up. She was sending us home and that was that. I was fully prepared to collapse and then let them deal with me, but Alison suggested it might not be helpful to do that, so I loaded her back into the car and aimed it towards home.

We didn't even make it out of the car park before Alison was screaming like there was a knife attacker in the back of the car with her. The calm lady that had suggested it best I not throw myself to the floor barely five minutes earlier had suddenly turned into devil woman. The screaming and name calling was definitely post-watershed stuff; I was told I needed to 'get the fucking car back in the pissing car park now', which was more difficult to do than you'd think: I was on a single carriageway road. Looking back, I can see it was a bad idea to try and do a three-point turn. I'm not that good at them at the best of times, but in those noisy conditions I ended up forgetting to turn the wheel before I moved the car again. I wasn't counting, but it was more like a thirty-seven-point turn by the time I finished. I also lost the indicator from the front nearside. By the time I got back to the hospital car park I didn't even bother paying for a ticket, or in fact finding a proper parking bay. I just wanted to get out of the enclosed space where all the screaming was going on. I suppose it was good practise for what was to come, although I suspect Charlie will have less violent intent behind his racket.

Nurse Miserable was at the door of the ward when we got back there; I'm not sure if it was the look on my face or the way Alison walked, but she didn't say anything like she'd been reeling off before. I think she must have realised she'd been stupid to send us away in the first place. I was mentally noting it all down. Heads were going to roll when I got out of there and managed to write a strongly worded letter.

They took us straight through to the ward, got Alison on the bed and went off to do something. It was the last we saw of them for two hours. Alison was going in and out of screaming fits, as were the other women on the ward. I went off a few times looking for a nurse, doctor, midwife, or indeed anyone that looked like they worked there. On the occasions that I found someone, they explained that it was extremely busy and that they'd be along as soon as they could. Every time I had to go back to Alison and tell her that I couldn't get her any pain relief and I couldn't help her, it was awful. I did think about going into the street and seeing if I could score some heroin. I've heard that's a good pain killer. Alison told me to shut up when I asked her 'where the fuck is everyone?' loud enough for the whole ward to hear. The next time I went looking for someone I saw several blokes in the same position as me, all looking up the corridor waiting for someone to come and help their partners.

I imagine the camps Hitler killed all the Jews in had a similar atmosphere to that ward. People just looking for help that never came, it was horrible feeling powerless to help. Things seemed to have slowed down for us over the past hour spent waiting. I don't know why, maybe that's what happens. Hollywood has a lot to answer for. They'd tricked me into thinking: get to the hospital, scream, push, baby – done. It isn't like that, though. Lord knows, it isn't.

There must have been a shift change, because all of a sudden we had staff all over the ward, all attending to the women. I could hear them tell the woman across from us to stop pushing as she wasn't in the labour room; she was wheeled away sharpish and within a couple of minutes they announced that she'd given birth.

It was our turn next. *It was happening.* Alison was taken into the delivery room and I followed shortly after; first I had to run and get a pasty from the machine at the other end of the six mile corridor. By the time I got back things were well underway. Legs were up, and Alison was sucking on the gas and air tube like her life depended on it. I asked if they were going to get the real drugs out once the contractions started, only to be stared at by the nurse.

'It's Alison's choice,' she told me, before making herself busy. I looked at Alison, who had her eyes scrunched shut and looked like she was in a lot of pain. I pointed to the green papers and asked the nurse to check the back page, where it clearly stated that I knew the birthing plan and would be asking for the pain relief. I'm still not sure how exactly it happened, but within a couple of seconds I was having a stand up row with the midwife.

If I had a button to push to win arguments I'd use it all the time. I don't, though, and the midwife did; she called in the cavalry and before I knew it there were three more midwives, and a couple of porters who looked like they smoked more than half the people in the mortuary did.

All I was asking for was the epidural that was on the birth plan and they threatened to remove me. I won in the end, as the head midwife told me the anaesthetist was on the way.

That wasn't a lie, but when she got there she informed us that she was only popping in for a chat before heading to A&E, where it was really busy. I asked what good she thought a chat would do my partner, who by this point had started crying. She just shrugged and went off, promising she'd be back.

The relationship between me and the midwife in the room never really improved; by the time the doctor started showing up, I'd been standing over a helpless Alison for about fifteen hours. The only thing of use I could do was give her sips of water when the contractions stopped. Things changed in the room when the doctor was there; people started milling about. The doctor knew what she was doing, she knew how to speak to me, and she gave very clear, direct and confident instructions to her team.

At that moment, at 4 a.m., I knew I was going to be getting a look at my son within the next hour. I started to feel a bit overwhelmed and the doctor asked if I was OK. I held my eyes as wide as they would go to make sure the tears didn't fall and maintained my male stance.

It was happening; mind you, the pushing had been happening for a while, although in the times that Alison could find the strength to talk, she complained about being too tired to push. The doctor seemed to breathe new life into us all. She told Alison what she needed her to do and she told her the time that it was going to take, which was something none of the other medical professionals had been prepared to do. A trolley was brought in containing all the things you'd expect to see on a trolley being wheeled into a birthing room, and some that I'd never seen before. It was just then that the doctor didn't *announce* that she could see the head, like I've seen on the TV, she asked if 'Dad' wanted to have a look at the head. I couldn't say 'no', but I wanted to. I'd managed to keep at the top end until then. I did have a glance, though, as I didn't want to disobey the doctor. If I'm honest, I couldn't really make out a head, it was a bit of a mess down there, and I am struggling to think about it now as I write.

Needless to say, as soon as I could I went back up to the top end and held the gas and air pipe for Alison. It was at such an angle, and the pipe was made of such tough tubing, that it was always wanting to bend the other way. I was getting cramp, but I couldn't not give her it. I was glad when Alison started screaming at me to 'get that useless fucking pipe' out of her face. It wasn't long after that, that the doctor got excited and told us that after three more pushes she was going to pull the baby out. The head was out at that point. I couldn't hear screaming, but I didn't have time to be worried because the doctor told us it was time; she grabbed a knife, cut something or other and then yanked my son out with a pair of forceps.

Then I heard the screaming. A little, white, soggy baby appeared and was handed straight to Alison, who looked in wonder at the child that was now in her arms. If I forget everything else in my life, the look on Alison's face when she first met our son is the one thing that I'd want to keep hold of. It was amazing. The first thing I noticed about the baby was his head. It was a funny shape. The shape of a cycle helmet. I was later assured that it was only like that for the birth and would go back to normal after a couple of days.

And I didn't faint, like Boris had suggested I probably would. He only said that because I did faint one time when I walked into the staff toilets after he'd been in there having one of his gentleman's sit downs.

I got shoved in the corner while everyone had a look at the baby, checked it over and cleaned up the poo he did pretty much instantly. It was then I thought I'd have a seat; I'd been on my feet for ages and they hurt. I sat down and stared at the floor, reflecting on everything that had just happened. It was an experience I'd never had before and at that moment in time I swore to myself I wouldn't do it again. I looked up and saw the doctor remove the afterbirth; it was then that I was sick in my mouth a bit. It was like the really awful part in the film, *Alien*. The doctor calling it 'breakfast' didn't help. And I had to swallow the sick.

Shortly after I was sick, Alison was also sick. I hadn't realised, but I'd fed her about three litres of water over the last few hours. The sick went on the baby a bit and that's when it was decided that I could have a hold of my son, which I did. He was so delicate. So small and so, so angry. I've never thought about what it must be like to be born, but I should think it's an absolutely terrifying experience. All of a sudden you're forced out of somewhere nice, warm and dark, with food on tap and no need to ever go to the toilet, into a bright room where someone in rubber gloves is just waiting for the chance to slap the shit out of you … literally. I bet it's freezing, too, like when you step out of a shower. He stopped crying for a while when I was holding him and went back to sleep. Then a nurse grabbed his feet and jammed a needle right into his heel which made him squeal for a minute before he went quiet. I wondered what they'd given him, thinking it must be some heavy duty shit for him to pass out straight away. We were assured he was OK and that it was just some harmless vitamin K that all babies are given. She then took him off me and got him dressed. I was able to see Alison; she'd finished having her downstairs sorted out and was padded up. She looked shattered. Shattered, but content. We were a family and without saying it, we knew we were linked together forever.

I got my phone out and took a couple of pictures, which I sent out to the people that had asked for them, then I asked if it was OK if I went home, as I was really tired and to be honest I wanted to get out of the way of the midwives. I knew that

Alison would be moved to the mother and baby unit soon and up there they'd have different staff. I started to feel a little bit guilty about the outbursts I'd made throughout the night due to the utter incompetence of the hospital staff, but deep down I knew that we'd been given a substandard service and I didn't want to find myself apologising for questioning it. Alison was fine with it and was going to start to see if she could start feeding Charlie when I left. There was someone there to help her do it and her motherly instinct had kicked in. I gave them both a kiss and headed outside to ring our parents and let them know the news. I rang my folks first and discovered that all four parents were together and waiting for the call before they opened some champagne. It was a bit weird, but I didn't really think too much about it. I just tried to remember where it was I'd left my car.

So that's how it happened. I'm now just about to leave the house and go and see my son again. I'd promised myself I'd get a decent sleep, but to be honest, I couldn't get to sleep as I was thinking about my son. I was thinking about all the things we're going to get up to in the years to come. All my hopes and dreams for him and us as a family. I was thinking about the family holidays I'd had as a child and how I hoped I'd be a good enough father to be able to recreate that for Charlie.

When I did wake up I had a message from Alison. It was a picture of Charlie and the message said, *'We love you, Daddy. Sleep tight. Visiting is at 10 a.m. Can you bring babygros? x'*

I'd only been out for a couple of hours, but my brain wasn't interested in letting me go back to sleep, so I hauled myself up and made a coffee before sitting down and waiting for 10 a.m. I was going to sit down and write a long complaint letter, but

155

I've decided that I'm not really interested in getting the inevitable reply that tells me they don't really care and that they haven't the money to make it better. It would just be a massive waste of time.

I'm going to see my son now.

OTHER TITLES

PETE SORTWELL

SO LOW, SO HIGH

Most people generally don't drink white cider for breakfast, don't use the aisle of Tesco as a toilet and don't steal from their family and friends. Simon Brewster does though. He's a doomed man. Living life day to day, stealing Edam balls and legs of lamb, ducking and diving his way from petty theft to dealer and back again. If he doesn't change his ways, he'll never see middle age, let alone old age.

He's seen his parents on their knees, crying, begging him to stop; he's been arrested by his former best mate; he's been hospitalised, all as a result of drugs and alcohol. It's just not enough to make him stop.

Simon lies to everyone, including himself. The truth is, he has no more idea why he does the things he does than you do. What he needs is a way out. But if such a thing exists, Simon hasn't had much luck finding it. He's powerless and his life is unmanageable to the point of insanity.

This is the story of Simon Brewster's last year using class A drugs. Join him as he crashes his way through police cells, courtrooms and display cabinets. One way or another, Simon will stop using drugs. But can the people that love him help him overcome his addictions before his addictions destroy him?

Available from Caffeine Nights Publishing.

THE COMPLETE IDIOT REVIEWS BOX SET

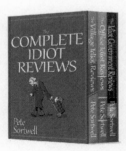

The first three 'Idiot' reviews books are now available from Amazon in e-book format as a handy box set.

PETE SORTWELL

ABOUT THE AUTHOR

Pete is 33 and lives with his wife, Lucie; daughter, Lilly; and their pet sofa, Jeff. He's been writing for just under three years and they've been pretty eventful; well, more eventful than he thought sitting on Jeff, typing, would be, anyway.

First published in the *Radgepacket* anthology with a story he'd written during month five of his new hobby, Pete's now featured in a total of ten different anthologies and has been amongst some very fine company. (Although he was the best in all of them, he knows that because both his mum and Jeff told him and they're both honest-to-God Christians ... possibly.)

Author of comedy e-books *The Village Idiot Reviews*, *The Office Idiot Reviews*, *The Idiot Government Reviews* and *More Village Idiot Reviews*, Pete has seen these books sell more than he ever thought they would, and he's hooked. *Dating in the Dark* is Pete's first self-published novel. His traditionally published novel, *So Low, So High*, was published by Caffeine Nights in June 2013.

Contact Pete:

Facebook:
https://www.facebook.com/pages/Pete-Sortwell/255907757862913

Twitter: @petesortwell

email: petesortwell@googlemail.com

13558326R00097

Printed in Great Britain
by Amazon.co.uk, Ltd.,
Marston Gate.